MORE
THAN A
CLEVER
STORY

The parables of Jesus are among the most quoted—and misunderstood—stories in the world. In this book, Brian helps us take a second and third look at these rich tales to find something deeper and more relevant than we could imagine. The real truths behind these stories are there for us to discover by reading a little more carefully. And the light they shed as we read attentively can change our lives.

—Paul Clark
Elder, Summit Church
Senior Consultant, Finding Great People

In all my years of ministry and biblical study, I have yet to meet someone with a purer and stronger love for the Word of God. The Lord consistently uses the way that Brian writes and teaches to bring me into a deeper understanding of biblical truth. What is even better is that the Spirit has gifted him to do so in such a way that it leaves you hungry and excited for more—more time with the Lord, more reading of the Scriptures, and more growth and transformation into the likeness of Jesus. This treatment of the parables does not disappoint; it is yet another example of Brian using his spiritual gifts for the "building up and equipping of the body of Christ."

—Josh Pederson
Assistant Director, 3Gen Ministries
Founder, Vox Bivium Discipleship School

MORE THAN A CLEVER STORY

WHAT JESUS WANTS YOU TO KNOW
ABOUT LIFE FROM THE PARABLES HE TOLD

Brian Onken

AMBASSADOR INTERNATIONAL
GREENVILLE, SOUTH CAROLINA & BELFAST, NORTHERN IRELAND

www.ambassador-international.com

More Than a Clever Story
What Jesus Wants You to Know About Life From the
Parables He Told

ISBN: 978-1-64960-153-7
eISBN: 978-1-64960-496-5

Scripture quotations are taken from the New American Standard Bible®, Copyright © 1960, 1962, 1963, 1968, 1971, 1972, 1973, 1975, 1977, 1995 by the Lockman Foundation. Used by permission. (www.Lockman.org) Italics are used in the New American Standard Bible to indicate words that are not found in the original language texts but are implied by it. Small caps are used in passages in the New Testament when the New Testament author is quoting an Old Testament passage or making a clear allusion to an Old Testament text.

Cover Design by Hannah Linder
Edited by Emily Caseres

AMBASSADOR INTERNATIONAL
Emerald House Group, Inc.
411 University Ridge, Suite B14
Greenville, SC 29601
United States
www.ambassador-international.com

AMBASSADOR BOOKS
The Mount
2 Woodstock Link
Belfast, BT6 8DD
Northern Ireland, United Kingdom
www.ambassadormedia.co.uk

The colophon is a trademark of Ambassador, a Christian publishing company.

To Sue

My wife, my partner in life, my best friend

Proverbs 18:22

CONTENTS

ACKNOWLEDGMENTS

FOR DECADES, I HAVE GROWN in my understanding of Scripture and, particularly, in my understanding of Jesus by reading texts together with others. Opening the Bible, reading a passage, thinking with others, discussing what we find in the text, and praying about those truths has been woven deeply into my relationship with God.

Recalling those years of reading and thinking and reflecting, my mind readily turns to others who have been on that journey with me. At the top of the list, I think of my family. For years, I would read Scripture with my children, Christopher and Kirsten (who are now both grown adults). Their ready and regular engagement with what we were reading and their willingness to ask questions and press in to see more clearly what was there in the Bible proved to be fruitful and encouraging. My wife, Sue, and I would often read something or discuss what we had heard in a Sunday message or wrestle together with a passage that she was going to teach in a women's study or that I was going to share in a local church. That rich family history has shaped my reading and my understanding of texts.

In addition, I have found a number of brothers in the Lord who have proved to be invaluable to me in growing to understand Scripture and to deepen my joy in Jesus. Paul Beyer, an InterVarsity staff member, was the one who first taught me to be genuinely attentive to the words of the text. Donald McDougal, a Talbot Seminary faculty member, led me to read the Greek New Testament and not simply translate words. Paul Voss of the Caribbean Ministry Association and Dan Thomas at Timberline Lodge both invited me to teach for their respective ministries and provided years of great discussions about the truths of Scripture.

Over the past decade, I have thoroughly enjoyed the fellowship and growth in the Word with a handful of brothers—both vocational ministers as well as laymen. Time with these men in the Scriptures continues to shape and encourage me. Bruce Gray, Bradley Cox, Ben Daniel, Nate Muse, Russ Muse, Paul Clark, Brian Briley, Craig O'Neal, and Stephen Enjaian have all been part of the journey; and the fruit of time with these men, and others like them, can be found in the pages of this book.

I also want to extend a special word of thanks to Lisa Mallory and Stephen Enjaian, both of whom provided valuable insight and comments as initial readers as these chapters were in process. Emily Caseres also deserves thanks for her competent editorial help in getting the manuscript into its final form.

SOME THOUGHTS ON READING THIS BOOK

"He was speaking the word to them, so far as they were able to hear it ... but He was explaining everything privately to His own disciples."

Mark 4:33-34

IN THE COURSE OF A conversation, the name of a famous person might come up. You could hear someone say, "Oh, I know him," or "Yes, I know her." When you press for more information, you realize that what that assertion meant was that the famous person was familiar to the one making the comment. It is not (typically) that the one who says "I know . . . " means that they are friends with the well-known actor or politician or athlete. It just means that they are aware of who the person is and, to some degree, aware of what makes that person famous.

When talking with people about Jesus, you will sometimes get a similar response. People say, "I know Him." For some, that means they have some awareness of Who Jesus was, maybe something about what He reportedly said and did, and perhaps a bit about

3

what "religion" teaches about Him. But for others, there is much more. When they speak about "knowing Jesus," they mean that they are familiar with Him the way friends know each other. They see themselves in a personal relationship with the living Jesus.

I raise this issue because of the approach taken in this book on the parables of Jesus. As you may know (or will come to learn as you read though this book), Jesus told these parables in a variety of settings and to a variety of listeners. Some of those He addressed were friends and followers; some were merely curious onlookers; some parables were shared in exchanges with those who were antagonistic toward Him. But in all the discussion of these parables, we will be responding to what Jesus said as someone who is in relationship with Him. In addition, the questions at the end of each chapter assume the readers of this book have more than a passing familiarity with Jesus. I approach these stories assuming the reader has a personal relationship with Jesus.

I am aware that some of those who pick up this book and begin exploring the parables of Jesus might not see themselves as having that personal relationship with Him. So for those who might not see themselves that way, I would like to address that. I want to clarify what I mean when I use that relationship language. And for the benefit of those readers who may wonder about their own life with Jesus, I want to address how they can enter that kind of relationship.

FOUR SIMPLE, BUT CRITICAL, IDEAS

Jesus spent three-and-a-half years in public ministry in the days of His incarnation, teaching and meeting the needs of those

He encountered. I cannot reduce all that He did and taught to a few paragraphs,[1] but I do think we can highlight a few critical elements of what He taught and what His teaching might mean for us. Without sounding reductionistic, perhaps we can focus on four key ideas:

1. LIFE IS FOUND IN RELATIONSHIP WITH JESUS.

This is not only a contemporary thing; for eons, people have been looking for "life." What does that mean? It is not simply about biological existence (a way of thinking about life) but about what we could call real life or significant life or even "eternal" life—the life that is worth living, the life that will last, the life that is meaningful.

If you listen to Jesus (reading His words found in the Gospels), it is clear He taught that life is only and finally found in relationship with Him. Here are just a few examples:

- "'Truly, truly, I say to you, the one who hears My word, and believes Him who sent Me, has eternal life'" (John 5:24).
- "'You search the Scriptures because you think that in them you have eternal life; it is these that testify about Me; and you are unwilling to come to Me so that you may have life'" (John 5:39-40).
- "'I came that they may have life, and have *it* abundantly'" (John 10:10).
- "Jesus then said to them, 'Truly, truly, I say to you, it is not Moses who has given you the bread out of heaven, but it is My Father who gives you the true bread out of heaven. For

the bread of God is that which comes down out of heaven, and gives life to the world.' Then they said to Him, 'Lord, always give us this bread.' Jesus said to them, 'I am the bread of life; he who comes to Me will not hunger, and he who believes in Me will never thirst . . . For this is the will of My Father, that everyone who beholds the Son and believes in Him will have eternal life, and I Myself will raise him up on the last day'" (John 6:32-40).

From these texts—and there are many more in the Gospels that we could turn to—it is clear Jesus taught that life is found in Him. To be in relationship with Him is to experience life in all its fullness.

2. RELATIONSHIP WITH JESUS IS NEEDED BECAUSE OF SIN.

Why might it be that life—in all its fullness and with all that means—can only be found in relationship with Jesus? The kind of life we are thinking about is the kind of life that can only come from the Giver of life—God. But there is a long-standing and widespread problem. Because of sin, people do not enjoy the kind of connection with God that would result in that kind of life.

People define sin in many ways—doing bad things, not living in a loving way with others, being selfish, hating others. But biblically—and to Jesus' way of thinking—sin is the orientation of heart and life that resists having God as the supreme Authority for life. And that orientation of life finds its expression in wanting life "on my terms."

To be living such a life—whether others perceive you as a basically "moral" person or not—will result in judgment, not life. To resist God's rightful place in life is to be a rebel against God's Divine right and Sovereign righteousness. Such rebellion deserves what all rebels ultimately deserve—death. Sin results in death—spiritual death—which is nothing less than being cut off from the source of real and satisfying life. To sin is to be cut off from God because of such rebellion.

When we listen to Jesus, it is clear that there are two experiences open to those on planet Earth—life with God or a life of separation from Him because of sin. John records that "Jesus answered them, 'Truly, truly, I say to you, everyone who commits sin is the slave of sin'" (John 8:34). And Jesus also adds, "'Therefore I said to you that you will die in your sins; for unless you believe that I am *He*, you will die in your sins'" (John 8:24).

The apostle Paul clarifies for us this problem of sin in his letter to the people in Rome, saying, "For all have sinned and fall short of the glory of God" (Rom. 3:23); and "For the wages of sin is death" (Rom. 6:23).[2]

This is more than a mere inconvenience; this is a serious problem. When the Bible speaks of the death that comes to all people because of sin, it speaks of more than physical death. The death in view is the judgment of God that falls on those who, in sin, are in rebellion to God. All people are afflicted with the soul disease of sin, and the consequence of that disease is to be separated from God—to not experience real and satisfying life.

3. JESUS RESOLVES THE SIN PROBLEM IN AND BY HIMSELF.

If we listen well to what Jesus taught, we can gain clarity about the connection between the problem of sin and why life is only found in Jesus. He came not only to teach about the kind of life that is available to those who trust Him, but He also explained why His coming was necessary for entering into that kind of life—life with God. Jesus said [referring to Himself], "'For even the Son of Man did not come to be served, but to serve, and to give His life a ransom for many'" (Mark 10:45).

What did Jesus mean that His life was going to be a "ransom"? The word refers to a payment made to set a person free. He knew that laying down His life through death was more than a good example; His death was going to accomplish something that would make it possible for others to experience a different kind of life. Jesus said, "'I am the good shepherd; the good shepherd lays down His life for the sheep . . . For this reason the Father loves Me, because I lay down My life'" (John 10:11, 17).

In anticipation of His soon-to-come death, Jesus offered a metaphor for His followers to understand what His death entailed. At the Last Supper, we hear His explanation: "And when He had taken a cup and given thanks, He gave *it* to [His disciples], saying, 'Drink from it, all of you; for this is My blood of the covenant, which is poured out for many for forgiveness of sins'" (Matt. 26:27-28).

After His death and resurrection, Jesus commissioned His followers to take the message of what He had done on behalf of sinful people: "And He said to them, 'Thus it is written, that the Christ [referring to Himself] would suffer and rise again from the dead the third day, and that repentance for forgiveness of sins would be proclaimed in His name'" (Luke 24:46-47).

Peter, one of Jesus' closest followers, explained His sacrifice this way: "For Christ also died for sins once for all, *the* just for *the* unjust, so that He might bring us to God" (1 Peter 3:18). Paul, writing to those who had found life with God through Jesus, also explained what Jesus had accomplished: "When you were dead in your transgressions [sins] . . . He [God] made you alive together with Him [Jesus], having forgiven us all our transgressions, having canceled out the certificate of debt consisting of decrees [of judgment] against us . . . and He has taken it out of the way, having nailed it to the cross [on which Jesus died]" (Col. 2:13-14).

Seeing that death—separation from God—is the only right and just consequence for sin, if people are going to have life with God, the sin problem must be dealt with. And Jesus is the One Who has dealt with it by serving as a Substitute. He gave His life, in death, as a ransom—a God-honoring and sufficient and satisfying life-for-life, in-our-place Substitute.[3]

4. STEPPING INTO THAT RELATIONSHIP IS A MATTER OF FAITH.

Given the need for life with God, the problem of sin, and what Jesus did in laying down His life as a Substitute, how does anyone step into that kind of life? What is the relationship between His death and the possibility of eternal life? How can we enter into life with God in view of Jesus' life and ministry?

The Bible describes entrance into that life as coming through "faith" or "believing."[4] A well-known passage of Scripture puts it this way: "'For God so loved the world, that He gave His only begotten Son, that whoever believes in Him shall not perish, but have eternal life'" (John 3:16). To "not perish" is to be freed from the death and judgment that falls on those who sin. To have "eternal life" is not simply to live for a long time but to experience the kind of life that the eternal God is inviting people into. To "believe" is to respond personally to Jesus and to abandon oneself to what He has done in living and dying and rising to provide, as a gift, this new life. John speaks of the results of either belief or unbelief:

- "He [Jesus] came to His own, and those who were His own did not receive Him. But as many as received Him, to them He gave the right to become children of God, *even* to those who believe in His name" (John 1:11-12).
- "'Truly, truly, I say to you, he who hears My word, and believes Him who sent Me, has eternal life, and does not come into judgment, but has passed out of death into life'" (John 5:24).
- "'Therefore I said to you that you will die in your sins; for unless you believe that I am *He* [i.e., the promised Deliverer], you will die in your sins'" (John 8:24).

To not believe in Jesus, to not trust Him and rely on His work on behalf of those who have sinned, leaves someone under judgment and still separated from life with God. As Jesus Himself explained to Nicodemus, "'He who believes in [Jesus] is not judged; he who does not believe has been judged already, because he has not believed in the only begotten Son of God'" (John 3:18).

In writing his Gospel, John explained why he made known to his readers what he had learned from Jesus: "But these [things] have been written so that you may believe that Jesus is the Christ [the promised, God-given Deliverer], the Son of God; and that believing you may have life in His name" (John 20:31).

WHERE THIS LEAVES US

This is what I long for you to know: life with God—the only full and real life—is available to any and all through what Jesus has done. Yes, your sin and my sin have resulted in alienation from God—His rightful judgment for our rebellion. But Jesus came from the Father to provide both a solution to the sin problem and a way into the fullness of life.

This life is experienced and entered into by faith—by believing in Jesus. A personal abandonment to Him—a giving up of any other solution or attempt to merit life through one's own efforts—is the only solution to death-dealing sin. All who welcome this message—the "Good News"—and depend solely on the sacrifice of Jesus as the grounds for relationship with God, enter into life!

It is my hope and prayer that you will not merely "know about" Jesus, but that you will enter into a genuine personal relationship with Him. You can call out to Him wherever you are. You can tell Him of your need for a sin solution and your awareness that He is the only One Who can resolve that problem. You can invite Him to give to you, as a gift that He purchased through His death and resurrection, this life with God you need. And He will do it!

DID YOU HEAR THE ONE ABOUT THE . . .

*"They were amazed at His teaching; for He was
teaching them as* one *having authority."*

Mark 1:22

FOR YEARS NOW, I HAVE lived in the Gospels. It is not that I
think that what we find in the Gospels is somehow holier or more
inspired than the rest of Scripture, but I continue to be fascinated
by Jesus—what He did (and still does), what He said (and how
those words can still be heard), and what difference that makes
in my life.

Books are written that discuss, reflect on, challenge, re-
imagine, and sometimes dismiss what Jesus said. That library of
volumes on the words and works of Jesus is a mixed collection—
some worth reading, others not so much. (Prayerfully, this volume
will fall into the worth reading category.)

My personal journey through the Gospels has been shaped by
a longing to hear Jesus' voice, to grow to understand what He said,

and to come to see how His words bring the life change I long for. I believe I have good reason to think Jesus' words can change a life.

Jesus pointed out that even though "'Heaven and earth will pass away, but My words will not pass away'" (Mark 13:31). He explained that to listen to and act on His words is like building a house on a solid foundation, but to not attend to what He says is to risk ruin (Luke 6:47-49).

On one occasion when Jesus was teaching "hard things" (something He does indeed do), some of those who were listening to Him took offense at what He had said (John 6:60). As a result, a number of those who had been following Jesus "withdrew and were not walking with Him anymore" (John 6:66). At that point, Jesus turned to His closest followers and asked if they wanted to leave as well. Peter's answer sums up a great deal about why I am so captured by Jesus' words: "'Lord, to whom shall we go? You have words of eternal life'" (John 6:68).

What did Peter mean when he said that Jesus' words are "words of eternal life"? I think there are a number of facets to Peter's confession. Jesus' words are in a category all their own. What He shares brings life. The things Jesus said are what lead His hearers into an experientially real life with the eternal God.

Those ideas—and more—are what fuel my desire to read and know and understand and take to heart what Jesus says. I am—and hope to continue to be—amazed by His teaching. In that amazement, I find what I need for life with God. That is the impetus for this book: to invite others in to listen to Jesus' words and be amazed and changed by them.

LEARNING TO LISTEN (AND READ) WELL

Matthew 13:34 tells us, "All these things Jesus spoke to the crowds in parables, and He did not speak to them without a parable." Even among those who profess no personal interest in Jesus, one can readily hear references to what Jesus said. His words are famous. He spoke in memorable and compelling ways. So even if one is not convinced His words are the words of eternal life, His words still command attention.

A significant portion of those words came in the form of parables. As recorded for us in the Scriptures, these stories Jesus told are widely known. The result is that many of the images found in Jesus' parables have passed over into common vocabulary and everyday conversation. Even when those quoting Jesus are not all that clear on what Jesus meant—and even when they are not aware they are quoting Him—they use His stories.

This happens every time someone says:

- "That prodigal son of mine."
- "She's a Good Samaritan."
- "Don't hide your light under a basket."
- "Count the cost before you begin to build."

On the surface, it might seem to be a good thing that Jesus' teachings have become part of our common vocabulary; but there is a downside. Our familiarity with the parables—or, at least, our sense that we are familiar with them—makes it challenging for us to listen well and read well. We can end up assuming that our pre-understanding about the characters or the issues pictured in the parables is correct.

We end up reading and talking about and thinking of Jesus' parables simply as "clever stories." We are, at times, amused or entertained, perhaps intrigued or puzzled by these memorable tales. And we end up thinking, *I got this! I know what He is talking about. Everybody does.* We read Jesus' parables like the colorful illustration or story a good teacher shares.

But is it possible that we are mistaken in our assumption that since we have some idea about what a particular parable might mean that we have listened to and understood Jesus well? Is it possible that how we read the parables results in our missing some—perhaps even a lot—of what Jesus wants to say to us?

Because of the large number of parables preserved for us in the Gospels and because of the widespread (but perhaps misguided) attitude that "I already know that" when it comes to Jesus' parables, there is a need to look at His parables with fresh eyes and open hearts.

Before we turn our attention to the first parable, we need to think clearly about just what a parable is. There are a number of formal and not-so-formal definitions that help us understand how a parable functions and how it differs from other figures of speech, like allegories.

The word *parable* in Greek is a compound word that refers to a "throwing alongside." One standard lexicon defines *parable* as "a placing of one thing by the side of another, juxtaposition."[5] You may have heard the old definition, "an earthly story with a heavenly meaning," which can hardly be improved upon. In other words, a parable may be defined as a simple story that, placed alongside our experience, illustrates a profound truth. Telling parables was Jesus' main way of helping His followers grasp spiritual truths. He was building a bridge from what His hearers would have been familiar with to some fresh insight He wanted them to understand.[6]

Simon Kirstemaker wrote: "Jesus drew verbal pictures of the world around Him by telling parables. He told a story, taken from daily life, using an accepted, familiar setting, to teach a new lesson."[7] William Barclay explained it this way: "Jesus gave us these cameo-like pictures we call parables so that the great ideas He wanted to teach might become comprehensible. He used earthly things to lead men's minds to heavenly things."[8]

Although each of these definitions (among others) is of some help in understanding how we should approach reading Jesus' parables, I believe there are a couple of very simple ways to think about a parable that aid us in coming to understand them.

In one sense, a parable functions like a joke. In both a parable and a joke, there is a story that is told in order to set up the punch line. While in a joke, the punch line is intended to elicit laughter, in the parable, the punch line is designed to provoke reflection and thought. But in both a joke and parable, the story being told is not usually entirely true to life. Although there may be a semblance to real life, in neither a joke nor a parable would we be listening well if we tried to make too much of the details of the story that are setting up the point.[9]

Just think. You are listening to a joke. (I know. The joke is hokey. But work with me here.) And the storyteller explains, "Two pieces of string walk into a café . . ."

In listening to this joke, if you interrupt all along the way because the details of the story do not make sense, you will never get to the punch line, and you will not get what is funny.

"Two pieces of string walk into—"

"Wait! How do pieces of string walk? And why are they going to a café?"

"Don't interrupt me. It's just a joke. So two pieces of string walk into a café, and the manager looks them over and says, 'Sorry, boys, we don't serve your kind here.'"

"Why did the manager call them 'boys'? How can you tell boy strings from girl strings?"

"Will you just let me get through the joke? The strings walk out; and as they head down the sidewalk, one of the strings says, 'Hey, I've got an idea to get into that café!'"

"Why is a string so bothered about getting into a café, anyway?"

"He's clearly not as bothered as I am trying to tell this joke! Let me finish. So the string starts twisting and tangling his head and pulling a few strands from the top. And he turns around and heads back into the café and—"

"So the string has arms, or what?"

"It doesn't matter! The string heads back into the café. The manager takes a look at him and says, 'Hey, aren't you that string who came in here a while ago I told to leave?' And the string replies—"

"Why doesn't the manager want strings in his café? What's wrong with strings?"

"Forget it! I'm done trying to tell you the joke."[10]

So, as we read and explore Jesus' parables, keep in mind that there are lots of details in the parable that are there, in one sense, to set up the punch line. Parables are not accounts of something that actually happened but, rather, a story with a point.

Another way to maintain a proper perspective on reading and understanding parables is to think of a parable like a verbal arrow. An arrow has a point—the business end of the arrow. But the arrow also has a shaft that gives weight to the point and feathers that help the arrow fly straight to the target.

In a similar way, a parable has a point (the business end of the parable), a shaft (the drama or movement in the story that propel the parable to the point), and feathers (the details in the story that help hold the parable on target). But just as it would be wrong to use the feathers or shaft of an arrow as if they were the business end of the arrow, so we need to be careful to not make too much of the shaft and feathers in a parable and, in so doing, miss the point.

In reading a parable of Jesus, when our attention is inappropriately focused on the shaft or feathers of the story, we end up drawing application from the details instead of from the point. If we are not careful readers, we can miss what Jesus is saying while creating our own spin on the story.

There is one more way to think about parables that helps distinguish between the point the parable is intended to make and the impact of the parable on the variety of people who listened to (or, in our case, who are reading) the parable.

When a pebble is dropped into a pond, you can see the pebble hit the water; and you can watch the waves extend out from the spot where the pebble made its impact. Once we understand the point of a given parable, we can tell where the pebble hit the water. But as we reflect on—and as Jesus' initial hearers reflected on—the point of the parable, the waves of implication may come on shore in different places in our lives. We may feel the impact in a variety of ways.

Although Jesus typically told a parable to respond to a particular issue raised by someone He was talking with or to point to an answer to a specific question He was asked, those listening were often a mixed multitude. The impact of the point being made would not have hit all the hearers in quite the same way—and we will find the same thing as we read His parables. We will not all feel the impact in quite the same way.

When reading or listening to a parable, it is also helpful to keep in mind that a parable lives in a particular setting.[11] In telling a parable, Jesus is not just hanging a clever story in the air. Typically, Jesus offers parables to answer questions, to address concerns raised, or to challenge a particular train of thought.

Parables were never spoken in a vacuum. In each instance that Christ spoke a parable, He was explaining some question or problem His hearers were facing. Each parable thus was designed to solve a problem or to answer a question.[12]

To understand a parable well, it is therefore necessary to pay attention to the setting of the parable. When we read a parable as if it is merely a stand-alone story, it becomes easier to overlook what Jesus is addressing and, thereby, overlook the point He intends to make (and, perhaps, miss the punch line!).

These overarching interpretive guidelines will be the basis of how we will approach the reading of Jesus' parables throughout this book. But there is one other issue that we need to touch on before we begin exploring particular stories.

HE IS NOT PLAYING GAMES

Some of the explanations I have read or heard of a parable seem to be quite complex and convoluted. I would not argue that all such efforts are valueless; but seeing as Jesus told His parables to average people and did not deliver them during deep, scholarly, philosophical debates, I think He intended His parables to be simple and clear.

I have heard some who insist that Jesus is purposefully trying to be difficult by telling parables. They argue that Jesus' intention is to present hard-to-understand stories in order to raise the bar for His hearers to see if they were really serious about listening to and learning from Him.

But I do not think Jesus sought to be obscure or obtuse. Although His parables were intended to be provocative, it would be counterproductive for Jesus to tell parables that were purposefully hard to understand or, even, incomprehensible to the average listener.

Our exegesis of parables, therefore, must begin with the same assumptions that we have brought to every other genre: Jesus was not trying to be obtuse; He fully intended to be understood.[13]

So when reading or trying to make sense of a parable, we should be looking for a clear "Aha!" We should be looking for the compelling and relatively simple point—even if the point He is making is intentionally provocative. The implications of the parable or the impact it could have on our lives might be deep and rich, but the basic story told should not be fundamentally cryptic. Jesus is not playing games with His hearers.

There is a passage in Matthew (with parallels in Mark and Luke) where some readers think Jesus is saying that He taught in parables for the express purpose of being *not* understood. But a closer look at that passage clarifies this is not what Jesus was saying.

> "Therefore I speak to them in parables; because while seeing they do not see, and while hearing they do not hear, nor do they understand. In their case the prophecy of Isaiah is being fulfilled, which says, 'YOU WILL KEEP ON HEARING, BUT WILL NOT UNDERSTAND; YOU WILL KEEP ON SEEING, BUT WILL NOT PERCEIVE; FOR THE HEART OF THIS PEOPLE HAS BECOME DULL, WITH THEIR EARS THEY SCARCELY HEAR, AND THEY HAVE CLOSED THEIR EYES, OTHERWISE THEY WOULD SEE WITH THEIR EYES, HEAR WITH THEIR EARS, AND UNDERSTAND WITH THEIR HEART AND RETURN, AND I WOULD HEAL THEM'" (MATT. 13:13–15).[14]

Reading carefully, it does not seem that Jesus is saying that He is speaking in parables *in order that those hearing Him would not understand* but only that in the case of some of those listening to Him, *they will keep on hearing but not understand.* It is not the case that Jesus is speaking in parables intentionally to preclude understanding. Nevertheless, although He is speaking in as accessible a way as a parable, some will continue to close their eyes to the truth.

The passage Jesus quoted is from Isaiah 6, recounting God's commissioning words to that prophet. God did not send Isaiah to the nation specifically for the purpose of ensuring that *the people would not understand.* God sent Isaiah with the realization that even in the face of his prophesying, the people's hearts would be hard; and they would not understand—until such a time as God would more radically intervene and move upon their hearts to awaken them to what He is doing.

In the parallel passage in Mark, Jesus follows up the quote from Isaiah (noted in the passage above) with a further explanatory word: "And He was saying to them, 'A lamp is not brought to be put under a basket, is it, or under a bed? Is it not *brought* to be put on the lampstand?'" (Mark 4:21).

What point is Jesus making? One would not bring out a lamp only to obscure its purpose of providing light. The implication is that it would be foolish to speak in parables if the speaking of the truth in parable form was only to obscure the light being providing in the telling of the parable.

Thus, although we might wrestle with the point Jesus is making in a parable, it would be wrong to conclude that He was purposefully trying to keep people from understanding. Although we might not immediately grasp Jesus' point (which could be due to our not reading the parable well or because of the challenging nature of the point Jesus is making), we must not settle into the idea that Jesus is intentionally being cryptic.

PUTTING THIS INTO PRACTICE

What lies ahead is an exploration of a selection of Jesus' parables. Reading them carefully, attentive to the guidelines laid out above, it is possible not only to understand what Jesus was saying but also to find life-giving and life-changing words for ourselves.

As we turn our attention to specific parables, a word of caution is necessary. We are going to read a parable, and then we are going to think well and think hard about what Jesus was saying—and, hopefully, see clearly what He intended in telling the parable.[15] We are going to do some analysis to ensure we are reading and hearing the parable well. And it is there we need to be cautious.

Jesus told memorable parables, and we are going to put them under a microscope. But like putting a beautiful butterfly under the microscope to see more closely its component parts, we can end up losing the beauty in the inspection process. That is not the intention; we are only seeking to read well. So we will step in close, look attentively at the story, and notice the setting and the details; but then we will step back to ensure we see the story as a whole. We do not want to lose the beauty of a parable in our exploration of what Jesus said.

Depending on the definition adopted by the Bible student and the method of counting used, the number of parables varies from one Bible teacher to another. This small volume does not cover all the Gospel passages where Jesus may be found teaching in parables. However, by exploring a select handful, we will learn how to read and understand Jesus' parables and, in so doing, come to be more captivated by His words and to be more amazed by the Savior.

CHAPTER ONE

SIMPLY PUT

NEITHER AN UNSHRUNK PATCH NOR UNFERMENTED WINE

"But new wine must be put into fresh wineskins."

Luke 5:38

MARIA IS A POSTULANT, PREPARING to learn what it will take for her to become a nun. As she is on that journey, the mother superior gives her an assignment—she is to serve as a nanny to seven children for a widower who lives near the convent. With Maria's arrival, everything changes in the widower's household, the home of Captain Von Trapp. The story is The Rogers and Hammerstein musical *The Sound of Music*.

A big part of the change in that family comes when Maria introduces music back into the lives of the children, and ultimately back into the life of the captain. In teaching the children to sing, she explains:

"Let's start at the very beginning; a very good place to start.

"When you read you begin with 'A, B, C;'

"When you sing you begin with 'Do, Re, Mi' . . . "[16]

From this simple beginning, Maria teaches the children the basic components they will need to make beautiful vocal music. And the rest, as they say, is history—or at least musical theater history. The children go on to sing some of the most memorable songs from the Rogers and Hammerstein repertoire.

There is some very reasonable advice in that simple lyric Maria taught the children—to learn anything, it is best to start at the beginning, to start with the basics.

In the introduction to this book, we touched on some of those basics concerning Jesus' teaching—fundamental ideas about how to approach the reading of a parable. In this chapter, we turn our attention to a couple of parables Jesus shared early in His ministry.

It makes sense to start with some simple parables—to see the basics of reading a parable played out in a simple way in a Gospel context. Like the Von Trapp children, we are going to learn the ABCs of reading parables. After having sung a simple song or two, we will gradually work our way through to some of the more challenging of Jesus' colorful stories in subsequent chapters.

Jesus had only been active in public ministry for a short time. He had been teaching in the area around Galilee, and those who heard Him were increasingly impressed with what they heard (Luke 4:14-15). He healed many sick people and delivered others from demonic spirits (Luke 4:40-41). Such activity resulted in His reputation spreading—and His coming to the attention of some of the Jewish religious leaders.

These leaders began to raise questions about Jesus. They could not quite make sense of Him and what He was doing (Luke 5:30–35). During one of His exchanges with some of these leaders, Jesus offered what serves as our first example:

> And He was also telling them a parable: "No one tears a piece of cloth from a new garment and puts it on an old garment; otherwise he will both tear the new, and the piece from the new will not match the old. And no one puts new wine into old wineskins; otherwise the new wine will burst the skins and it will be spilled out, and the skins will be ruined. But new wine must be put into fresh wineskins. And no one, after drinking old *wine* wishes for new; for he says, 'The old is good *enough*'" (Luke 5:36–39).

Jesus was addressing the concern some religious leaders had about Him. They were resistant to what He was saying and doing, so Jesus intended to help them with their difficulty. The way He sought to do this was to offer them these two short parables. But in order to make sense of these parables, we need to take a step back to ensure we see the bigger picture.

YOU'RE DOING WHAT?

Two incidents preceded the telling of these two parables. It is those two incidents—exchanges with the religious leaders—that provide the broader context for Jesus to share these two stories.

As Jesus' ministry grew, large crowds followed. As those people gathered, they often stayed with Jesus—listening to Him and watching what He was doing. Many of them were healed or delivered from oppressive spirits.

What would it have been like to be in that crowd? What would you have wanted? There was a hunger to be with Him, to be where He was, and to do all one could to remain in His presence.

It was in that setting (Luke 5:29-32)—crowds hanging out with Jesus—that the religious leaders raised a question. They wanted to know why Jesus was eating with "tax collectors and sinners" (Luke 5:30). Tax collectors are not particularly popular in our day; but in Jesus' day, they were even less popular. Very few Jews would have had a kind word to say about a tax gatherer. These revenue collectors worked for Rome, making it possible for Rome's presence and rule to spread.

The tax collectors had taken up Rome's invitation to collect monies from their own people—they had bid for that right. Who would like to befriend a neighbor who had bid for the privilege of collecting money from others only to turn the payments over to the oppressive regime that had conquered the nation?

Not only were the taxes themselves a burden, but the tax collector would also make his living by charging what he could over the amount he promised to turn over to Rome. For obvious reasons then, tax collectors were an unpopular bunch.

Lumped in with them were the "sinners." It's not that the religious leaders thought that there were some Jews who were immune to sin. Those identified as sinners were those known to be habitual sinners, perhaps even making their living in a sinful way (like prostitutes, perhaps). These were people with a sinful reputation.

Jesus was eating and drinking with tax gatherers and sinners—shocking! It is not that He was a tax collector or a man with a sinful reputation, but He *was* sharing a table with those kinds of people.

Enjoying a meal with someone was more than sitting for a few minutes next to another person the way we might do in a fast food restaurant or sharing a table in a crowded coffee shop. To eat with someone—to share a table—would have been a sign of acceptance, putting oneself on par with those with whom one ate. To enjoy a meal with tax collectors and people with a sinful reputation would have been unthinkable to the leaders who raised the issue with Jesus. Those were the people who were hanging out with Jesus—and those were the people the religious leaders could not imagine identifying with in any way.

But be careful how you think about that. We should not see these religious leaders—the Pharisees and the scribes—simply as a gang of wicked hypocrites or social snobs. Although Jesus does end up in conflict with some of these leaders,[17] it would be wrong merely to see them as the "bad guys."

By and large, the Pharisees were devout, pious, and religiously and politically conservative teachers of Jewish life. Although Jesus later will call some of those who had come to test Him hypocrites (Matt. 23:13-15), this does not mean that all Pharisees were hypocrites. They were not all maliciously out to get Jesus.

Then we have the scribes. The scribes were copyists. They were responsible for maintaining and copying the scrolls containing the Scriptures used in the Jewish religious services. Every Scripture scroll—whether in a local synagogue or in the temple in Jerusalem—was a handwritten copy. Daily, regularly, continually, the scribes would be making copies. Their careful hand-written work was preserved on animal skins, prepared to serve as the paper of the day. But those skins lacked durability, so the copying process was ongoing. Because of their work, the scribes would have become very familiar with the text of Scripture. And therefore, they were looked to as those who could answer questions about the Scriptures.

Like the Pharisees, some scribes did end up in conflict with Jesus. But as with the Pharisees, it would be an overstatement to conclude that the scribes were, by and large, self-serving hypocrites maliciously opposing Jesus. In their desire to maintain traditional Jewish life and affirm the priority of the Scriptures in the life of the Jewish community, the Pharisees and scribes would have struggled with anything that they felt undermined those commitments. They ended up with methods and strategies for holding on to Jewish culture, life, and religion so as to preserve the nation and to honor the God of Israel.

In a world where Roman influence and culture was spreading, the idea of sharing life with those who did not seem to strive for Jewish purity in thought and practice would be inconceivable to them. That is why the Pharisees and scribes were shocked when Jesus ate with those they saw as potentially undermining the Jewish way of life they dedicated their own lives to preserving. They wrongly concluded that Jesus' sharing in life with such people meant that Jesus not only approved of their life choices but also that He was unconcerned about holiness and preservation of the nation. The Pharisees and scribes had adopted a habit of life—undoubtedly well-intentioned—that Jesus did not adopt. And this was what prompted the conflict they had with Jesus.

Fasting was the second concern that led up to these parables. The religious leaders had embraced fasting as a spiritual habit, and they could not understand why Jesus and His disciples did not do the same (Luke 5:33). The word "fasting" does not appear in any specific command in the Old Testament. Nevertheless, the idea of fasting has some Old Testament roots.

As part of the celebration surrounding the Day of Atonement, the people were called to "afflict their souls" (Lev. 16:29).[18] This expression appears to refer to an actual fast, seen in the way the phrase is used elsewhere in Scripture.[19] This reference to the Day of Atonement is the one place where God instituted a regular annual fast.

There are a number of times when an individual or leader either fasted or called others to join in a fast. Jehoshaphat called the nation to a fast and to seek the Lord (2 Chron. 20:3). Ezra invited others to pray and fast as they looked to God for safety (Ezra 8:21). Nehemiah fasted when he learned of the condition of the city of Jerusalem as he sought to discern God's will (Neh. 1:4). Esther asked others to fast and pray for her at a point of crisis (Esther 4:16). In each of these occasions (and others like them) fasts were undertaken with a view to a particular need or to respond to a particular life situation. So although there was no specific command to regularly fast—apart from the one annual occasion—fasting was not unknown.

Perhaps rooted in such Old Testament thoughts, in their passion to pursue a life of holiness, the Pharisees fasted weekly.

They did not require everyone to fast the way they did, but they did think fasting was an appropriate spiritual discipline—good for the individual's soul and good for the nation.

It was hard for them to imagine that Jesus and His disciples would not join them in this regular habit. They wrongly concluded that since Jesus was not fasting the way they were, He must not be concerned about His spiritual life or the spiritual condition of His followers.

These two concerns—eating with those they would not have shared a meal with and not adopting regular days of fasting as a spiritual discipline—led the Pharisees and scribes to question Jesus' perception of spiritual truth. He did not fit with what they saw as standards for holiness. And it was their discomfort with Jesus that was the setting for His response—and for these two short parables.

SIMPLE—BUT UNFAMILIAR—PICTURES

Jesus put these two parables together in the same immediate context. Both of them are intended to make the same point. They are paired and given in response to Jesus' developing trouble with the religious leaders, and these two clues help to make sense of what Jesus sought to communicate.

Jesus first talked about cloth: "'No one tears a piece of cloth from a new garment and puts it on an old garment; otherwise he will both tear the new, and the piece from the new will not match the old'" (Luke 5:36).

In our day, ripped jeans and torn clothes might pass for cutting-edge style. But that has not always been the case. The owner of a favorite garment—thread-worn and torn—might have sought to repair a tear or fix a hole. But no matter how scarce the fabric on hand, no one would have thought it wise to rip a new garment to mend an old garment. You would end up with an unwearable new garment and a poor fix for the old. Your situation would be worse than before the patch job.

The other image comes from winemaking: "'And no one puts new wine into old wineskins; otherwise the new wine will burst the skins and it will be spilled out, and the skins will be ruined. But new wine must be put into fresh wineskins. And no one, after drinking old wine wishes for new; for he says, *The old is good enough*'" (Luke 5:37-39).

Fresh grape juice would have been sewn up tightly in an animal skin; the animal skin would serve as the container. As the juice permeated the skin, the skin would become both flexible and relatively moisture-tight. As the juice fermented, gasses would be released, stretching the skin. When the time was right, the skin would have been opened; and the wine enjoyed. But used skins would have been valueless when it came to making another batch of wine. They had already stretched as much as they could; old skins would have been of no value in the fermenting of new wine. You would only try that once—and lose both the old wine skin and the new wine.

And what of those who have enjoyed old wine? Seeing as new wine was not yet fermented (it had not ripened with age), the flavor would not have developed. No one would have chosen new wine over old. If you had tasted both, you would not have mixed them—and you would not have opted for the new.

For Jesus' hearers, both of these parables would offer familiar pictures. Both share the same "punch line" (as explained in the introduction to understanding parables). There is a simple "aha" to these stories: *The new and the old do not typically fit together.*

These stories are not sets of instructions about what someone should or should not do, although those hearing the stories would have known how foolish it was to either patch an old garment with a new patch or put new wine into used wineskins. Jesus was responding to the concern of the religious leaders. Keeping in mind the tip of the arrow, we need to ask the next question: how do these parables address the religious leaders' concerns?

ON TARGET

We now have our basics. We have our A and our B, and we need to move on to the C for our first parable exploration. Understanding a little about the conflict Jesus was beginning to have with these religious leaders, seeing the immediate context of His remarks, and having some sense of what is pictured by the parables, we can now ask, what is the point? How does the punch line speak to the situation? As we step into the moment, watching as the religious leaders raise their concerns, listening to their questions, and paying attention to Jesus' response, how are we to understand what Jesus is doing?

One of the risks we face as contemporary readers of the Gospels is that we can readily import into an exchange like this all we know about Jesus from other passages of Scripture. But the religious leaders did not have that benefit. They had only begun the journey of getting to know Him. They knew little about where the story is going; they grasped very, very little about what Jesus was all about. We might see implications of Jesus' words that would not have been—and could not have been—part of what these religious leaders heard in Jesus' parables.

As contemporary readers, we know that Jesus' message will ultimately supplant the approach to life with God that was at the heart of the Pharisees' and scribes' religious experience. We know that a "new covenant" would, in a few short years, be instituted that would fulfill and overshadow the covenant approach, rooted in the temple sacrifices, that was woven into the very fabric of the lives of these men.

So when we hear "new patch" or "new wine," we might assume that Jesus is speaking of all that "new stuff," which we know is going to break into the world. All of that *is* true. It is just unreasonable that such an understanding is what Jesus had in mind when He first shared these parables with some religious leaders who were having trouble understanding Him.

Throughout the Gospels, Jesus meets people where they are— whether those who would become His friends and disciples or those who are cautious and critical of Him. He does not have unrealistic expectations for them. He does not speak to them in such a way that they will not be able to grasp what He is saying. So what would those who first heard these words of Jesus understand Him to be saying? That is where we need to anchor our thoughts about these parables. That should be our starting point—what we can affirm, minimally, that His hearers could have understood.

We have the narrative setting for these parables. We have some sense of what Jesus pictured in these two stories. Given that, we can readily think through what could well have been going on in the minds of those who heard these stories.

"What should we do? This Jesus, this new rabbi, does not understand our ways. He does not value the traditions that have been passed down to us for hundreds of years."

"We are only trying to preserve what we most value, to hold on to our Jewish ways in the face of Roman rule."

"But this Jesus—He shares the table with Jewish traitors who take our money and give it to Rome."

"He eats with those who have no regard for our traditions or our desire to preserve true holiness."

"Weekly, we give ourselves to times of prayers and times of fasting. We only seek what is best for the nation. We are fighting for the way of life we have always known."

"And this Jesus, He seems to ignore our traditions, our way of life, our longings to preserve a holy life for the people of God."

And Jesus told them a parable, saying, "'No one tears a piece of cloth from a new garment and puts it on an old garment; otherwise he will both tear the new, and the piece from the new will not match the old. And no one puts new wine into old wineskins; otherwise the new wine will burst the skins and it will be spilled out, and the skins will be ruined. But new wine must be put into fresh wineskins.'"

"New wine in new wineskins—everyone understands that!"

"Yes, the new and the old do not fit together. But why remind us of that?"

"This Jesus—He does seem to know the Scriptures. He does teach in the synagogues. The people have embraced Him."

"Could it be that He is not seeking to undermine our tradition—the faith of our fathers Abraham, Isaac, and Jacob—but only intends to clothe it in new garments?"

It is not a hard thing Jesus is seeking to do. He wants to lead these religious leaders to consider the possibility that what He is doing does not entirely undermine what they long for. He wants them to consider the possibility that there could be a fresh way to "make wine." The idea is not hard to grasp—it is just that it has not occurred to them with regard to their life with God.

A VERY GOOD PLACE TO START

Whenever and wherever we turn to Scripture, there are three fundamental questions we need to keep in mind. In order to not hijack the meaning of a text, we need to ask:

1. What does this passage say? What are the words?
2. What does this passage mean? What is the intent of the author?
3. What does this passage mean for me?

Although we want biblical passages to intersect our lives and speak to us, we cannot begin with "What does this mean for me?" It is much too easy to overlook what a passage actually *says*—and would have meant to the original hearers—if we *begin* with the implications of a passage for us. After we have listened well to the passage and sought to grasp what Jesus intended to say to the religious leaders, we can wrestle with the implications of these parables for our lives.

We are not living in first-century Israel. We are not waiting for the coming of the promised Messiah. We are not living under an oppressive Roman rule. We are not fighting to hold on to traditions that we are convinced are necessary for living holy. Oh, wait—maybe we do struggle with that last one!

Jesus was not entirely rejecting all the religious leaders longed for or held on to. Some of them did become His followers. There was—and is—continuity between Jewish life before Jesus' entrance into the world and life after His death and resurrection.

These parables about new and old should not be read either as Jesus' summary dismissal of all things Jewish or as a simplistic condemnation of all the Pharisees and scribes were doing. But they do highlight a tension that everyone who meets Jesus faces. Jesus may not do things the way we think He should, the way we are accustomed to having things done.

Although our life situation is not identical to that of these religious leaders, the point of the arrow prods us in a similar way. Jesus will not always do things in the way we think He should. Jesus' approach to life may not turn out to be the way we would prefer. That might not seem like much of a life-altering truth. But it is a place to start—a place to start in understanding parables and a place to start in understanding how Jesus speaks to people.

Jesus gives these religious leaders a simple, easy step. "Is it possible that there is something new and fresh happening in what I am doing?" He is not driving to the full revelation of His person, and nature, and mission. He simply suggests, "You do understand that sometimes the new will not fit with the old?" Jesus is kind, approachable, understandable.

Watching Jesus, listening to Him, I realize how often I bump up against this very thing. I need to hear the simple message of these parables often.

I can remember stepping into married life with a clear picture of what I thought a "Christian marriage" was supposed to be. But as those early months unfolded, I came to realize that my expectations and perspective were not the same as Jesus'. He wanted to do something different, something that struck me as "new." It was not a complete overthrow of all I understood to be included in a God-honoring view of marriage, but it was a re-adjustment—a re-adjustment that did not immediately fit with my way of thinking.

Over years of ministry in various church settings, I see that what we embrace as "how church should go" is, sometimes, only our preferred way of doing life. We have learned a certain approach to worship, to prayer, to teaching, to ministry. In our desire to preserve "the purity of the Gospel," we tenaciously hold on to those approaches. But Jesus does not always do things the way we have come to insist on.

Those who have grown up with "altar calls" cannot understand how anyone can get saved without a call to "go forward" (even though there is no example of such things in the New Testament). Those who have a particular experience with the Spirit are confused when others do not appreciate and seek that experience (even though such experiences are not mandated for all believers in the New Testament).

Jesus nudges the Pharisees and the scribes to re-think what they prize. The essence of what they long for is going to be preserved, while the traditions might be altered. The new thing might be challenging, but it will not be inconceivable. And if they are willing—and if I am willing—Jesus will gently, clearly, graciously, and purposefully lead those who are listening into fresh experiences of kingdom life.

REFLECTING ON THIS TRUTH
FOR PERSONAL REFLECTION:

1. We can over-read Jesus' words, thinking that He is saying more than is really there in the text. These parables are simple. Jesus is not explaining all He has come to do but only giving the Pharisees and scribes an easy step forward in their journey with Him. How does it feel to realize that Jesus takes this kind of approach with them? What are the implications for you in your life with Him?

2. Where are the places in life where you are feeling a little tension between how you would like to do things and where you think Jesus might want something a little bit different? Talk with Him about the "new thing" He is doing or addressing in your life. Let Him help you make a re-adjustment in your thinking. Hold loosely to your traditions and hold tightly on to Him.

3. As you continue to read and explore Jesus' parables, ask the Spirit to grant you understanding. Invite the Spirit's help to hear Jesus' words in fresh ways—to not read into these parables anything that Jesus was not saying and to hear well what He was saying.

FOR GROUP DISCUSSION:

1. Why is it important to be attentive to the context in which we find a parable of Jesus? How does recognizing that help in understanding these two short parables?

2. If we do not begin by thinking that the Pharisees and scribes are "bad guys" intent on opposing Jesus from the start, how can that help us when we read about His interactions with them?

3. Where do you find yourself being challenged by the "new thing" Jesus is doing in your life? What can help us be more open to Jesus' tendency to do things quite differently than we might initially think He should?

CHAPTER TWO

WHAT DID HE SAY?

THE SOWER, THE SEED, AND HIS INTENTIONS

"Behold, the sower went out to sow."

Mark 4:1

FOR YEARS, I DID STAGE magic—I performed illusions for the sake of entertainment. My undergraduate degree was in theater; my emphasis was performance; and my focus was on magic for the stage.

Over the years, I have cut people in thirds (and, yes, restored them), levitated my lovely assistant into the air only to have her vanish, and delighted young and old with feats of legerdemain. But there was no real magic—it was well-thought-out trickery, all for the joy of fooling and being fooled.

Often, when friends and acquaintances discover my familiarity with prestidigitation, they will ask me to explain something they have seen some other magician or trickster do—whether live or on stage. Almost invariably, as they describe the mystery they would like me to unravel for them, a common problem arises: they don't describe accurately or fully what they thought they saw.

I'm well aware of the phenomenon. In fact, as a practicing magician, I would count on it. You see, at the heart of all good stage magic is the science and art of misdirection. If the viewer's attention can be controlled and directed, then the stage performer can get away with seeming magic on the stage. When I hear a friend describe something he saw, I see the evidence of misdirection at work. Nearly every recounting confirms that the watcher only saw what the magician wanted him to see because of how his attention was directed.

At the heart of this problem (for viewers) and the benefit (for performers) is the difficulty we have in paying attention to multiple things at the same time. Many people take it for granted that they can multitask well; they intuitively think that they can be truly mindful of multiple focal points at one and the same moment. But this just is not true—and a successful magician counts on that.

Years ago, a clever experiment was conducted that confirmed what magicians have long known about this problem of inattentiveness. The project was quite simple and became the starting point for the book named after the experiment: *The Invisible Gorilla*.[20]

In the experiment, viewers were shown a video of two teams of people—half in white shirts, half in black shirts. While watching, they were asked to count the number of passes made by the white-shirted players. Halfway through the video, a student dressed in a full gorilla outfit walked behind the players, faced the camera, and then walked off. After watching the video, when viewers were asked how many passes were made, most of them got the number right. But when asked if they had seen the person in the gorilla suit, nearly half did not notice the gorilla-suited addition. The misdirection of counting the passes kept them from seeing something fully in view.

So why do we begin this chapter on one of Jesus' parables by thinking about misdirection and invisible gorillas? Are Jesus' parables examples of misdirection? Is Jesus doing something tricky when He tells these memorable stories? Of course not.

The misdirection that happens when we read Jesus' parables has more to do with what we bring to the reading of the text rather than what Jesus is doing or saying. As touched on in the introduction to this book, the familiarity many of us have with Jesus' parables can leave us being attentive to the wrong things when reading or listening. And as a result, we end up not seeing the gorilla in the scene. We can read and look and—because our attention is on what we *think* Jesus is saying rather than on what He *actually* said—we can miss what might be critical.

Aware of this tendency, what can we do when we come to a familiar parable? A few things are helpful:

1. Try not to assume you know what the parable is about before you have listened well.

2. Make sure you give attention to the setting of the parable for clarity about what Jesus is addressing by telling the parable.

3. Do not start with a "spiritual application" of the parable; let the story be heard with simple impact.

With those thoughts in mind, we can turn our attention to one of Jesus' most well-known parables with a willingness to listen as if we have never heard it before.

> He began to teach again by the sea. And such a very large crowd gathered to Him that He got into a boat in the sea and sat down; and the whole crowd was by the sea on the land. And He was teaching them many things in parables, and was saying to them in His teaching, "Listen to *this*! Behold, the sower went out to sow; as he was sowing, some *seed* fell beside the road, and the birds came and ate it up. Other *seed* fell on the rocky *ground* where it did not have much soil; and immediately it sprang up because it had no depth of soil. And after the sun had risen, it was scorched; and because it had no root, it withered away. Other *seed* fell among the thorns, and the thorns came up and choked it, and it yielded no crop. Other *seeds* fell into the good soil, and as they grew up and increased, they yielded a crop and produced thirty, sixty, and a hundredfold." And He was saying, "He who has ears to hear, let him hear."
>
> As soon as He was alone, His followers, along with the twelve, *began* asking Him *about* the parables. And He was saying to them, "To you has been given the mystery of the kingdom of God, but those who are outside get everything in parables, so that WHILE SEEING, THEY MAY SEE AND NOT PERCEIVE, AND WHILE HEARING, THEY MAY

HEAR AND NOT UNDERSTAND, OTHERWISE THEY MIGHT
RETURN AND BE FORGIVEN."

And He said to them, "Do you not understand this
parable? How will you understand all the parables?
The sower sows the word. These are the ones who are
beside the road where the word is sown; and when they
hear, immediately Satan comes and takes away the word
which has been sown in them. In a similar way these are
the ones on whom seed was sown on the rocky *places*,
who, when they hear the word, immediately receive it
with joy; and they have no *firm* root in themselves, but
are *only* temporary; then, when affliction or persecution
arises because of the word, immediately they fall away.
And others are the ones on whom seed was sown among
the thorns; these are the ones who have heard the word,
but the worries of the world, and the deceitfulness of
riches, and the desires for other things enter in and
choke the word, and it becomes unfruitful. And those
are the ones on whom seed was sown on the good soil;
and they hear the word and accept it and bear fruit,
thirty, sixty, and a hundredfold" (Mark 4:1-20).

How does Mark begin this account? "[Jesus] began to teach
again by the sea." If we had been journeying through Mark,
it would be clear that this was not Jesus' first time at the Sea
of Galilee and not the first time He had been teaching the
crowds. But as Mark records his account for us, the episode he

introduces here is the longest section of Jesus' teaching up to this point. Mark has told us that Jesus is a unique teacher (1:22); he has shown us the crowds that gathered to hear Jesus speak (2:2). But we have only heard a few paragraphs from Jesus—until this portion of the Gospel.

Jesus got into a boat and had the boat pull a short distance from the shore. That way, the large crowd could all the more easily hear Him. Mark tells us Jesus taught them many things; we are not given all that Jesus said. But Mark highlights a few things out of that message by the lake.

The parable Mark recounts—just a simple story—does not seem to be so very complex. It is a story of a farmer who sows seed. For people steeped in an agrarian way of life in the land around that lake, it would have been understandable. So do not begin by thinking about how you might prepare your corner garden or what you might do if you were going to lay sod in your backyard. That would not be what was in Jesus' mind nor what His original hearers thought. Listen to the story as Jesus taught it.

CAN YOU PICTURE THE SCENE?

Think about what Jesus said as He told this parable. The sower scattered seed. He is the only actor in the story; he is the only character that does anything. (It is helpful to keep that in mind; parables tend to be built around the actors.)

What does the sower do? He simply scatters seed indiscriminately; he broadly casts the seed. Do not push against that idea because it is not the way you might do it. Do not overanalyze why the sower might do it this way because it does not immediately make sense to you. Listen and learn.

In the parable, the sown seed falls on a variety of kinds of soils. In describing the soils, it is clear that in the indiscriminate sowing, some is not going to bear fruit. But it is also clear that some will bear some fruit—although all of the fruitful soil is not pictured as bearing the same yield. If you just listen to the parable, the punch line is obvious: when seed is indiscriminately sown, some will likely bear fruit.

Now Jesus' closest followers, having listened, came to ask Him about the parable. It wasn't just the twelve; Mark tells us that others also came to raise questions. (Kind of like we do when we read it. "What does this mean? What are you saying?")

Although Jesus provides more details in the explanation that followed, the point of the story seems to be the same. Even with the perceived allegorical explanation[21] Jesus offered, the point is not obscured. Widely scattered seed falls on widely different soils; and when some of that scattered seed falls on good soil, it will, invariably, bear fruit.

Do not miss the simplicity of the parable. If we are paying attention, we can readily dismiss some things that Jesus is *not* saying in teaching this parable. Jesus is not talking about how bad soil might become good (even though some Bible teachers will talk about that idea in explaining this parable). He is not giving instructions about what one must do to not end up being poor soil (although in a desire to make the application of this parable more personal, some will talk about that). He is not telling a parable about strategic Gospel advancement and the need to target how kingdom ministry should be done. His story focuses on the sower sowing seed.

This parable is familiar to many—even many who do not understand Jesus or His life and ministry. This parable has been unpacked by countless teachers and pastors—often well, but sometimes in a less-than-simple way. Given how this parable is commonly handled, the idea that Jesus' point is this simple can seem trite or overly simplistic. But the simple truth presented might actually be exactly what Jesus was offering.

In replying to His disciples' question, Jesus provided not only some further explanation but also a few statements that clarify what Jesus intended to communicate in telling the parable.

> As soon as He was alone, His followers, along with the twelve, *began* asking Him *about* the parables. And He was saying to them, "To you has been given the mystery of the kingdom of God, but those who are outside get everything in parables, so that while seeing, they may see and not perceive, and while hearing, they may hear and not understand, otherwise they might return and be forgiven" (Mark 4:10-13).

Between the telling of the parable and the explanation, Jesus spoke to those who "began asking Him about the parables." If we are reading attentively, what He said next should be a bit surprising: "'To you has been given the mystery of the kingdom of God, but those who are outside get everything in parables.'"

Can you imagine how this would be heard by those who came to ask about the parable? They came, apparently, because they wanted some clarification. And Jesus told them they had "'the mystery of the kingdom.'"²² Others only got a parable, but those who came had the secret—or so Jesus told them.

But they came because *they did not understand*. How can that be reconciled with the statement that *they had the secret and that the mystery was theirs*?

Some readers conclude that the mystery of the kingdom is Jesus Himself. Since the inquirers came to Him, that must be the key. But Jesus does not withdraw from those who did not come to ask. And He did not say "those outside do not get Me"—He said the only thing the others have is a parable. It would not seem that "having Jesus" (as critical as that is to life in the kingdom) is what Jesus had in mind here. The contrast Jesus is highlighting is between having the mystery (or the secret) of the kingdom and only having a parable.

That drives us to ask, what was true about the inquirers that was not true about the others? What difference can we detect in them that might provide some insight into the mystery of the kingdom and the point of this parable?

There is just one thing, from the text, which distinguishes the inquirers from the others. The inquirers wanted to know more. The inquirers apparently thought that what Jesus had said was important, so they wanted to make sure they understood. They responded as if Jesus' words mattered. Perhaps that is the mystery, the secret, of the kingdom: responding to what Jesus said as if what He said is the most important thing.

The focus of the parable is not so much on becoming the right soil. The focus is on the sower sowing what is most important—the seed. The parable pictures what Jesus was doing—not as an allegory but as a helpful illustration. The sower sows seed—that is the thing that matters—and some of that sown seed will ultimately bear fruit.

Jesus was indiscriminately sowing words as He told parables. But only some responded as if those words mattered. It is not that those who did ask Him fully understood—they came because they did not understand. But they did not blow off what Jesus said. They did not just hear the words; they listened attentively.

AN OLD TESTAMENT ANCHOR POINT

In replying to the disciples' question, Jesus quoted a passage from the Old Testament book of Isaiah: "'While Seeing, They May See And Not Perceive, And While Hearing, They May Hear And Not Understand, Otherwise They Might Return And Be Forgiven'" (Mark 4:12).

God spoke those words to the prophet Isaiah as He was commissioning the prophet to carry out a ministry of proclamation among the people of Israel. The nation had turned from the Lord; they were not whole-hearted in their pursuit of Him. So, God was sending Isaiah with a message.

In explaining to Isaiah what He wanted for him, the Lord let the prophet know that there was not going to be an immediate and complete response to the message he was commissioned to deliver. The people would see but not fully grasp Isaiah's message; they would hear what he said but not completely understand. They would be exposed to the word of God through the prophet of God, but Isaiah needed to be aware that this did not mean that they would all turn and repent and be restored. God was letting Isaiah know that he needed to proclaim the message God had given him without regard for the response—or lack thereof—of those he was being sent to speak to. In other words, Isaiah would have to indiscriminately proclaim God's message. And the Lord wanted him to know that the proclamation did not mean that all the seed sown would bear fruit.

God was not telling Isaiah that He was sending Him with the express purpose of the people of Israel not listening and not understanding. (In fact, Isaiah asked the Lord about the lack of response he should anticipate, and the Lord explained to him that He was going to work in the hearts of the people so that, ultimately, repentance would come.)[23]

Jesus was not saying that He spoke in parables for the express purpose of having His hearers *not* understand. But Jesus was clarifying that He was doing the thing that was most important— He was indiscriminately spreading the word.

Jesus, in fact, made it clear that He was *not* speaking in parables in order to make things hard to understand. He offered a simple metaphor to make that point: "And He was saying to them, 'A lamp is not brought to be put under a basket, is it, or under a bed? Is it not *brought* to be put on the lampstand? For nothing is hidden, except to be revealed; not has *anything* been secret, but that it would come to light'" (Mark 4:21-22).

It is reasonable! No one lights a lamp and puts it where it will do no good. Jesus is not speaking to the crowd in a way that would do them no good. Even if the sense of the parable is "hidden" (after all, He speaks of the "mystery" or "secret" of the kingdom), the ultimate intent was *not* to keep hearers from the truth but to entice them to respond to the truth—the way that those who came and asked for understanding did.

LIVING IN THIS PARABLE

Jesus' words matter. Responding, in some way, to what He says is at the heart of the mystery of the kingdom. This is what is evident in the narrative in which this parable is found. The secret is not necessarily coming to full understanding of everything we hear from Him. Those who came and asked for clarification clearly did not understand everything they heard. The secret is responding to what we hear as if what He says matters.

Listen to how Jesus drew His explanation of this parable to a close: "'If anyone has ears to hear, let him hear.' And He was saying to them, 'Take care what you listen to. By your standard of measure it will be measured to you; and more will be given you besides. For whoever has, to him *more* shall be given; and whoever does not have, even what he has shall be taken away from him'" (Mark 4:23-25).

Everyone has ears, so what did Jesus mean in speaking about having "ears to hear"? Listen well! Pay attention to what you hear. He elaborates by calling His disciples—and us—to "take care what you listen to." And then He spoke about those who would be given more. To what was He referring? There are some, in the narrative where this parable is found, who were given more—those who came and asked. They got more words from Jesus. They did not fully understand, but they did respond as if what He said mattered. And as a result, He told them more. Their "standard of measure" was to give attention to what He had said; and in responding that way, they were given more.

As you sit reading this chapter and wrestling with what Jesus said and what it means for you, you are living in this parable. Even if you do not fully grasp all that happened in this exchange recorded for us by Mark, the fact that you are thinking things through, reflecting on Jesus' words, asking Him for clarification, and wanting to know more means you have the mystery of the kingdom! You are responding as if what Jesus says matters.

REFLECTING ON THIS TRUTH
FOR PERSONAL REFLECTION:

1. As Jesus taught, it was His desire that His hearers understand. And as we listen and read, it is our desire to understand. However, there will be times that we might not fully understand something that Jesus says—whether because of our lack of experience, our inattentiveness, or our misperceptions. But that should not keep us from the secret of the kingdom. What have you learned about the kind of response that you could make to what Jesus says, even when you may not fully understand?

2. Can you recall a time or a passage where you found it hard to understand something you felt Jesus was saying to you? How did you respond? Did you simply acquiesce, assuming you would not get His point? Did you press in asking and looking for more? What is your typical habit when brought

face to face with some word from Jesus that you do not immediately understand?

3. Although Jesus is not physically present with us in the way He was when He taught at the Sea of Galilee, He is not absent from our lives. He promised to be with His followers (Matthew 28:18-20; John 14:18); He is present with us. Knowing that—and knowing that the secret to the kingdom is responding to His words as if they matter—spend some time talking to Him. Ask Him to show you where you have been dismissive or inattentive to something He has said to you. Ask Him to give you ears to hear!

FOR GROUP DISCUSSION:

1. What is the biggest challenge you face when you are reading a very familiar parable (like the one in this chapter)? What can help you read with "fresh eyes" and listen well to what Jesus is saying?

2. When you first hear that there is a "secret" (or "mystery") to the kingdom, how do you think about that? If "secret" does not mean something that has to be uncovered (as in a detective story) but something that is revealed, how does that help you understand what Jesus was explaining in telling this parable?

3. In what way do we—when we are reading and discussing this very parable—have "the secret of the kingdom"? How are you going to respond to this parable?

CHAPTER THREE

NOT WHAT HE THOUGHT

A PRIEST, A LEVITE, AND A SAMARITAN

"But a Samaritan . . . when he saw him, felt compassion."

Luke 10:33

ROXANNE IS THE YOUNG, BEAUTIFUL woman who is the center of affectionate attention in Edmund Rostand's play *Cyrano de Bergerac*. Two men love her—a young musketeer named Christian, and Christian's commander, named—as you may have guessed—Cyrano. The play's intrigue swirls around the interactions between these three. Christian has some feelings for Roxanne, but he lacks both the depth of heart and the language fit for winning her heart. Cyrano has strong feelings for Roxanne with both a depth to his love and a richness of language fit for wooing her—but he has an enormous nose that makes him both loathe his own looks and resign himself to never being the object of such a woman's love.

In a strange twist, Christian confides in Cyrano his feelings for Roxanne; and Roxanne confides in Cyrano her blossoming interest in Christian. When Christian attempts to write Roxanne of his affections, he shares these nascent thoughts with Cyrano. The big-nosed and big-hearted man concludes the language Christian has used is entirely unfitting for such a recipient as Roxanne. Christian prevails upon a not-entirely unwilling Cyrano to help him write to her. The result is letters (lots of them, ultimately) written by Cyrano are sent by Christian to the unsuspecting Roxanne.

Roxanne is taken by the letters. They touch her deeply. Real affection stirs in her for the man who wrote these elegant missives. But she wrongly thinks—through no fault of her own— that the one she is growing to love is Christian. When he is killed in a battle, she mourns the loss of her love and decides to become a nun.

In subsequent years, Cyrano pays daily visits to Roxanne— ostensibly to cheer her up but, in truth, to be in the presence of the one he loves. He continues to hide his true feelings and the secret that died with Christian, until the very end. In a tragic turn, Cyrano dies in Roxanne's presence, the victim of an ambush on the way to see her.[24]

So why this long recitation of Rostand's classic play? Because the play turns on a problem often encountered in reading parables: misunderstanding who is speaking and what is actually being said. Roxanne misunderstood that the letters that captured her heart were from Cyrano and the expressions of affection were his, not Christian's.

Roxanne assumed—perhaps with good warrant—that the letters and the words were Christian's. She assumed she knew who was speaking and what he was saying to her. In a similar way, we sometimes assume—with much less warrant—that we know to whom Jesus is speaking and what He is saying when we listen to His parables.

The imagery of the parables has, in large measure, passed into the common culture. As a result, they have become so familiar, we often *assume* what is being communicated with the result that we might end up missing what Jesus really intended to say.

When we turn to Jesus' parable about the "good Samaritan," we have to recognize it could be hard for us to hear this parable in the way Jesus intended because of the way "good Samaritan" has passed into common usage. We speak of someone being a "good Samaritan." There is even a "Good Samaritan Club" for travelers on the road. The image, for us, seems pleasant and encouraging. But in Jesus' telling of the parable, the Samaritan would not have been identified as "good"—even in light of what he is pictured as doing.

A little background will help. The account of Jesus' encounter with a woman at a well in Samaria in John 4 provides a helpful clue. John reminded his readers, "Jews have no dealings with Samaritans" (4:9). To put it mildly, the two groups did not get along. The Samaritans were those who lived in the land between the Roman provinces of Galilee in the north and Judea in the south. They were descendants of those who had been left in the land of Israel when Assyria and Babylon conquered the Jewish state and scattered many of the Jews toward the close of the Old

Testament history.[25] Those foreign powers imported other alien people into the land. Many settled in the area that came to be known as Samaria, intermarrying with the Jews who had not been sent into exile. The result was a mixed race and, ultimately, a mixed religious life.

When the Jews who had been exiled were allowed to return to Israel during the time of the Persian kings, Jerusalem was rebuilt and the temple service reinstated.[26] But those faithful Jews who had returned were unwilling to let the Samaritans join in the reinstated worship, feeling that their compromise during the time of the exile disqualified them. So those living in Samaria established a separate place of worship.[27] Without the temple and without the priesthood, an alternative was adopted. The Samaritans did embrace the Old Testament, and they found some justification for what they were doing—much to the dislike of the Jews who lived both to their north and to their south.

Thus, when Jesus told a parable with a Samaritan as a key figure, He was painting a picture with anything but pleasant colors. None of His hearers would have been thinking kind thoughts about the Samaritan in the story—and no one would have imagined a "good Samaritan club" as either possible or desirable. With a little of our culturally accumulated shine knocked off of the Samaritan, perhaps we can hear the punch line of Jesus' parable a bit better.

IT DIDN'T COME OUT OF THE BLUE

For us to read and hear this parable well, we have to give attention to why Jesus told this story. It does not just hang out there on its own. The parable was offered as part of a conversation

Jesus was having with a "lawyer"—a student and teacher of the Old Testament Law.

> And a lawyer stood up and put Him to the test, saying, "Teacher, what shall I do to inherit eternal life?" And He said to him, "What is written in the Law? How does it read to you?" And he answered, "YOU SHALL LOVE THE LORD YOUR GOD WITH ALL YOUR HEART, AND WITH ALL YOUR SOUL, AND WITH ALL YOUR STRENGTH, AND WITH ALL YOUR MIND; AND YOUR NEIGHBOR AS YOURSELF." And He said to him, "You have answered correctly; do this and you will live." But wishing to justify himself, he said to Jesus, "And who is my neighbor?"

> Jesus replied and said, "A man was going down from Jerusalem to Jericho, and fell among robbers, and they stripped him and beat him, and went away leaving him half dead. And by chance a priest was going down on that road, and when he saw him, he passed by on the other side. Likewise a Levite also, when he came to the place and saw him, passed by on the other side. But a Samaritan, who was on a journey, came upon him; and when he saw him, he felt compassion, and came to him and bandaged up his wounds, pouring oil and wine on *them*; and he put him on his own beast, and brought him to an inn and took care of him. On the next day he took out two denarii and gave them to the innkeeper and said, 'Take care of him; and whatever more you spend, when I return I will repay you.' Which of these three do you

think proved to be a neighbor to the man who fell into the robbers' *hands*?" And he said, "The one who showed mercy toward him." Then Jesus said to him, "Go and do the same" (Luke 10:25-37).

If we are not attentive—like Roxanne missing the clues as to who really wrote those letters to her—we will misconstrue this parable. What do we need to notice? To begin, we need to look carefully at what prompted Jesus to tell this story.

A lawyer came to Him—not an attorney the way we might conceive of it; think of a professional student of the Old Testament Law. But this lawyer did not come with a genuine, heartfelt question about something he would like Jesus to clarify. The lawyer asked his question to put Jesus to a test[28] (10:25). We are not told exactly what this test was, but his was no idle question.

So, in what way was this a test question? Luke does not explain, but there are hints in the question the lawyer raised. To ask Jesus about what could be done to inherit eternal life opens up the possibility that if Jesus did not answer in precisely the way the lawyer (and those who sided with him) wanted, Jesus could be charged with overlooking some important facet of the Old Testament Law. After all, the teachers of the Law categorized over six hundred rules and laws the faithful were supposed to keep in order to live holy and, thus, qualify for eternal life.

The second intriguing thing about the question is that the lawyer asked what he could do "to inherit" life. Think about that for a moment. What does one do to inherit? Really, there is only one way—you have to be born into the family. An inheritance is not something you work to obtain; you do not earn an inheritance. It is something that gets passed to you—if you are an heir.

So, there were two awkward facets of the lawyer's question: He wanted Jesus to select some prominent instruction out of all the Old Testament, and he wanted Jesus to explain how to get in on something that could only be inherited. Both aspects of the question set Jesus up for a possible trap. It is not likely that Jesus missed the test nature of the lawyer's question. In replying to the man, Jesus was not simply answering the man's question. Wanting to engage the man in conversation, Jesus framed their conversation by what He asked. He replied to the man by asking for a starting point: "What is written in the Law? How does it read to you?"

"How does it read to you?" That is an interesting way to ask His question. Jesus was probing. He did not want the man to give a thoughtless answer; He wanted the man to think for himself. "As a lawyer familiar with the Law, how do you understand what is necessary for inheriting eternal life?"

Conversant with the Law and the teachings of the rabbis, the lawyer had a ready answer. He quoted from Deuteronomy; including a passage referred to as the *Shema*.[29] The lawyer's reply emphasized a passionate and wholehearted love for God and a proper care and affection for one's neighbor. The lawyer simply repeated the heart of the prayer that a faithful Jew would have prayed every day. It was a safe answer, a good starting point.

Jesus used the lawyer's starting point as the starting point for His own reply. He affirmed the fitness of the lawyer's response and then simply said: "Do this—love God supremely and love others appropriately—and you will live."[30]

Unfortunately, many who are familiar with the parable that follows draw a simple conclusion: Jesus is telling this lawyer that he only has to do these two things—love God and love others— and he will merit or earn or deserve life with God. It is as if Jesus were giving the lawyer a formula for inheriting eternal life. But as we saw at the very beginning of this book, eternal life with God cannot be merited. So what does this mean for Jesus' response to a test question? Did Jesus not recognize the question was a test? Did He not care to answer appropriately? Was He willing to let the man wrongly conclude that doing certain kinds of loving things would, in some way, procure eternal life? Is it not more likely that Jesus' response—and the parable that follows—is much more provocative than is often assumed?

But there is something more. There is another question that leads us to the parable. The lawyer was not fully satisfied with how Jesus had replied. If the test question was designed to trap Jesus, it seemingly did not work as intended. The lawyer is not put off by the exchange he was having with Jesus; he wanted to learn a bit more. However, in the lawyer's follow-up question, his lack of sincerity and genuineness is evident: "But wishing to justify himself, he said to Jesus, 'And who is my neighbor?'" (10:29).

By asking this question, the lawyer emphasized the lesser of the two commandments he himself had quoted. He overlooked love for God and only asked about love for one's neighbor. And, specifically, the lawyer did not ask about *how* one was to love a neighbor but only wanted to know *who* qualified as the object of neighbor love.

We are not told why the man did this. We could speculate a bit. Perhaps he felt he already was appropriately loving God. Maybe he did not see loving God to be as challenging as loving other people. Or it could have been that seeing there was just one God, the call to love God was clear; but seeing as the man likely knew many other people, clarifying the call to love one's neighbor left him with a feeling of ambiguity.

But we are also told something else: The man wanted to "justify himself." He wanted to make the case that he was a good guy; that he was right before God. He wanted the acknowledgement that he was, in fact, "in." Apparently, he thought if he could be sure that he was loving his neighbor, then he could assure himself—and prove to others—that he was living life right.

It was in reply to this self-justifying question that Jesus told the parable. That was the context for the parable. The lawyer asked a disingenuous question in order to trap Jesus and followed it up with a question by which he intended to justify himself. But Jesus does not play such games. He will not allow Himself to be caught in a trick question, and He will not help someone on his or her quest for self-righteousness.

This must mean that when Jesus offered the parable of the good Samaritan, He was not falling into the trap of offering a formula for achieving holiness before God for those who want to justify themselves. The parable cannot simply be a set of instructions for getting right with God—despite how it is often understood. So, go back and re-read the parable again—this time attentive to the context of the conversation. Keep in mind that Jesus is not giving the lawyer steps to follow to "inherit" eternal life. Keep in mind that Jesus has no intention of helping the lawyer "justify himself." With those thoughts in mind, what strikes you about the parable?

THE QUESTION THAT DRIVES TO THE POINT

What is clear is that the context for this parable begins with a series of questions:

Lawyer: "Teacher, what shall I do to inherit eternal life?" (A question the man asked to trap Jesus.)

Jesus: "What is written in the Law? How does it read to you?" (A question Jesus asked to encourage the man to reflect on what he was asking.)

Lawyer: "And who is my neighbor?" (A question the man asked to justify himself.)

In response to that question, Jesus told the parable—the one we know as the parable of the Good Samaritan. Remembering that the parable is *not* an account of something that actually happened, the basics are nevertheless memorable.

A man is beaten by thieves. Various religious people—a priest (who would have been responsible for sacrifices in the temple) and a Levite (who would also have been involved in the temple worship in Jerusalem)—are pictured as passing by the man. Then a Samaritan comes by and not only tends to the man's wounds but also arranges for the man's convalescence. (And as was noted earlier, the interaction between a Samaritan and a Jew itself would have been a shocking turn in the story.)

When Jesus came to the end of the parable, He asked the lawyer one final question that helps clarify what Jesus was focusing on. "Which of these three do you think proved to be a neighbor to the man who fell into the robbers' hands?"

Did you notice the disconnect? Jesus did not specifically answer the lawyer's question. The man had asked who he should think of as his neighbor; Jesus asked who was neighborly. The man wanted to have an answer that would allow him to justify himself; Jesus' question points in a different direction.

Jesus was reorienting the conversation: "The issue is not about identifying who is your neighbor. The issue is what kind of man you are." Do not overlook the distinction made in the parable between the Levite, the priest, and the Samaritan. Although they are labeled in that way, the thing that distinguishes the Samaritan from the others is *not* that he did something (although he did). What is pictured for us is clear—both in the story and the answer the lawyer gave to Jesus' question. The Samaritan had compassion; he was the one who was merciful. The parable underscores that the issue is not just acting in a neighborly way but being a certain kind of person—having a heart that is right.

The lawyer was not focused on *being* a certain kind of man but simply *doing* the kinds of things he believed would earn him a standing with God. In other words, the lawyer asked a number of wrong questions. The parable was Jesus' way of rephrasing the entire conversation.

Listen again to the way Jesus closed out the exchange: "'Which of these three do you think proved to be a neighbor to the man who fell into the robbers' *hands?*' And he said, 'The one who showed mercy toward him.' Then Jesus said to him, 'Go and do the same'" (10:36-37).

Now we might think—if we are not listening carefully—that Jesus just told the man to "go and do" something that would allow him to "inherit eternal life" and that would make it possible for him to "justify himself." But if we have listened carefully, it becomes clear that Jesus' closing charge is, in truth, impossible for the man.

The lawyer wanted rules to live by; he asked about what was required to merit eternal life. The lawyer wanted limits on how he lived with others; he asked about who qualified to be shown gracious love. And Jesus asked him to think about the kind of man who "proved to be a neighbor." Jesus wanted him to think about a particular *kind of person* and not about a specific *set of tasks*. So when Jesus told the man to "go and do the same," it would have been clear to the man—and to us when we read carefully—that Jesus gave this man a call that would be impossible to carry out by himself.

In this passage, Jesus twice told the man to "do" something. In verse twenty-eight, in reply to the lawyer's identification of what the Law proscribes, Jesus said, "Do this." In verse thirty-seven, in reply to the lawyer's identification of who was genuinely neighborly, Jesus said, "Do that." After the first call to "do," the lawyer had a question—one wherein he sought to justify himself. After the second call to "do," the lawyer apparently has no reply. But given what we have seen of this lawyer, it would seem there could have been an appropriate follow-up question: "How can

I possibly go and do the same when I am more concerned with justifying myself than I am with being the right kind of person?"

DO YOU SEE YOURSELF?

When we read an exchange between Jesus and someone else in Gospels, it is helpful to see ourselves in the story. Not that we are to wrongly assume we *are* that other person, but trying to find how we connect with or identify with the one in conversation with Jesus is beneficial. The sad thing about this particular exchange is that we often identify with the lawyer without realizing the full implications of what Jesus is saying.

We hear the exchange, and we wrongly assume that the questions the lawyer asked were legitimate and sincere. Because we ask the same questions in our relationship with Jesus, we tend to assume the best of the lawyer. And then, listening to the parable, we conclude that Jesus simply wants us to be nice and helpful to others so that we, too, can "inherit eternal life."

The point of the parable is fairly straightforward. It is a picture of the right kind of person. The parable points to a person with a right heart. But the lawyer clearly does not have a right heart. He is seeking to trap Jesus. He self-righteously wants to justify himself. And my fear is that when we read the parable as if it is simply a set of instructions, we *do* identify ourselves with the lawyer—in all of his self-righteous, self-justifying, merit-based life with God.

When we read the parable of the Good Samaritan as if Jesus wanted His hearers—wants us—to simply do nice things for people we would not normally choose to associate with so that, in doing such things, we can earn our standing before God, we have missed the point of the parable! Like Roxanne, we have drawn the wrong conclusions from what we have read.

What might be a better response to this parable? Rather than, "Oh, I can do that!" perhaps the more appropriate response would be, "You want me to do what? You want me to be *that kind of person?*"

That response would suggest that we really felt the impact of the punch line of this parable. Rather than concluding Jesus is offering a simple formula for inheriting eternal life by doing good, we would conclude Jesus was underscoring the need to find life by becoming (with His help) a radically different kind of person. If this truth had come home to the heart of the lawyer, he might have realized it is not enough to find the limits of who I get to act loving toward; I will have to really love others. And seeing as he had only asked about neighbors, he might also come to realize something else—it is not enough to find the limits to how I should act toward God; I will have to really love Him.

It is a bit startling that Luke does not tell us anything about the lawyer's response to Jesus' final words to him—no question, no evidence of sadness or gladness, no recorded response of any kind. The exchange ends with Jesus' words; and we are just left hanging, wondering how the lawyer might have responded. And perhaps that is Luke's intention (under the leading of the Spirit). If the lawyer did not respond in any particular way to Jesus' words— leaving that awkward silence hanging in the air—Luke might have wanted his readers to feel that as well.

When I think about the exchange between Jesus and the lawyer this way, I am reminded of a conversation I had with a friend some years ago. He was having some challenges in his marriage, as many couples do from time to time. He came to me, explaining, that "he did not feel love for her." I had heard similar things from others in the midst of the challenges of growing in marriage. And he asked me, "What can I do to show my wife that I love her?" That strikes me as a question very much like that asked by the scribe.

Loving someone (such as your spouse) is not fundamentally a matter of doing the right things but having the right heart. If you genuinely had true affections (a heart shaped by the work of the Spirit in you), you would not ask that kind of question. The doing would be a natural outflow of the orientation of the heart. So my response to my friend in answer to his question about what he could do was simple: "Love her." And that threw him back on the core of his problem: He did not need some task to follow through on; he needed his heart to be changed.

I think that is what was going on in the exchange between Jesus and this scribe. Jesus was not, fundamentally, giving the man something to do but presenting to him a picture that might just cause him to realize that the problem was deeper than behavior—it was a heart problem.

A REAL-LIFE APPLICATION

Luke helps us in a way that the lawyer was not helped: He immediately follows up the account of the parable of the Good

Samaritan with an exchange that took place between Jesus and some of His friends.[31]

> Now as they were traveling along, He entered a village; and a woman named Martha welcomed Him into her home. She had a sister called Mary, who was seated at the Lord's feet, listening to His word. But Martha was distracted with all her preparations; and she came up *to Him* and said, "Lord, do You not care that my sister has left me to do all the serving alone? Then tell her to help me." But the Lord answered and said to her, "Martha, Martha, you are worried and bothered about so many things; but *only* one thing is necessary, for Mary has chosen the good part, which shall not be taken away from her" (Luke 10:38-42).

Could it be that by following up the parable of the Good Samaritan with this account, Luke is helping his readers understand something essential?

The contrast between Martha and Mary is clear. Martha was busy with many things; not necessarily valueless things, but apparently not the essentials—at least from Jesus' perspective. Doing all those seemingly good things—preparing for company, making sure the needs are met, not overlooking what could be done—was distracting Martha from the one necessary thing. The contrast is between someone committed to *doing* and someone given over to just *being*.

The lawyer appeared to be concerned with what to do—what to do to inherit life, how to choose who was his neighbor so he could do the right thing and justify himself. He overlooked the call to love God and wanted to know how to limit his loving actions. He was not concerned with being one who loved God and others—he just wanted to know which hoops to jump through to be good enough. And Jesus told a parable to awaken him to the reality that life is not about doing loving things but being caught up in loving—loving God and loving others. And Luke follows that up with Jesus' exchange with two of His friends that underscores that contrast.

Martha was busy with so many things. She wanted Jesus to acknowledge she was doing good; she wanted Jesus to make Mary do what she was doing. Does that not look like "justifying herself"? But Mary sat attentively listening to Jesus. And we might rightly ask, "Which of these two do you think proved to be someone who loved Jesus?"

And it is right there that I think I catch a glimpse of myself. It is so easy for me to settle into making the case—to myself and to others—that I am a "good guy." I want the acknowledgment that I am okay, that God must accept me because I am doing the right things. Like the lawyer, I want Jesus to simply give me a short list of steps I can take to assure myself that I am righteous. Like Martha, I not only want Jesus to affirm the good I am doing, but I also want Him to call the attention of others to what I am doing.

But the parable and Jesus' questions and the exchange He had with Martha all point to an implied but essential question: do I really love God? Have I settled for doing stuff in place of being a lover?

REFLECTING ON THIS TRUTH

FOR PERSONAL REFLECTION:

1. It is so easy—particularly when we are reading a parable that we have heard before—to miss the point Jesus is making because we draw our conclusion too quickly, before we have really paid attention. What have you learned about how Jesus wants to engage with this lawyer (and with us) by paying better attention to the parable of the Good Samaritan?

2. It is clear that Jesus was aware that this lawyer's questions were not entirely sincere. Nevertheless, Jesus did not dismiss him. How does it help you in your relationship with Jesus to know that not only does He see behind the questions you might ask but that He still graciously engages with you, even when you are less than genuine in your approach to Him?

3. At the heart of this exchange is the issue of the lawyer's heart. Once we understand the parable correctly, it becomes clear that Jesus is not extending a call to merely "do the right thing." Where do you struggle with the challenge of having Jesus call your attention to what is going on in your heart and not merely thinking of Him as concerned about the stuff you do?

FOR GROUP DISCUSSION:

1. How have you heard the parable of the Good Samaritan (before reading this chapter)? Where does the emphasis often fall?

2. Why is it critical to notice Luke's commentary about why the lawyer came and why he asked the questions he did? What happens in our reading the parable if we do not grasp what gave rise to Jesus telling this story?

3. When rightly understood, what do you find most challenging about this parable? How does reading it well move the parable from being a nice story about doing good things to something that can actually press us to think more honestly about living into the life Jesus wants for us?

CHAPTER FOUR

FINDING YOURSELF IN THE MIDDLE

THE MAN WITH A FRIEND AT MIDNIGHT

"Friend, lend me three loaves, for a friend of mine has come."

Luke 11:5

IT IS PRETTY OBVIOUS. CERTAIN things just go together. I had a great picture of that when I was on vacation with my wife in Mexico.

The beaches were warm and inviting. The hotel had the amenities we wanted and needed. We had enjoyed a few days of Mexican hospitality and food. But one evening, we decided we wanted something other than typical Mexican fare. So, we decided to look for options. And we found a great alternative—a Japanese steak house not far from the hotel.

We had visited this same chain at home, so we anticipated something familiar. And, for the most part, it was. As is typical

When we are reading and wrestling with what a passage means, it is often critical to keep in mind where we find the passage. The particular setting will help us make sense of what we are reading. If we ignore the context, we might end up with a view of the passage that does not really fit the author's intention or the author's flow of thought.

We are going to turn to another parable—one that may be familiar, one that might, on the first reading, seem obvious in its intent. After looking closely at the parable, we will step back a bit and take a look at the setting. In doing that, we might come to see that the setting influences how we understand the parable far more than we might have thought when first we read the parable.

As we have noticed, parables do not "walk on all fours." That is, parables are neither allegories nor straightforward statements of the way things are. Jesus tells parables to stir thought, to make a point, or to engage His hearers. There is a primary point in every parable, but we should not assume that all the details in the parable are either a snapshot of real life or correspond to something true. Keep that in mind as we turn to one of Jesus' parables about prayer.

> Then [Jesus] said to them, "Suppose one of you has a friend, and goes to him at midnight and says to him, 'Friend, lend me three loaves; for a friend of mine has come to me from a journey, and I have nothing to set before him'; and from inside he answers and says, 'Do not bother me; the door has already been shut and my children and I are in bed; I cannot get up and give you *anything*.' I tell you, even though he will not get up and

give him *anything* because he is his friend, yet because of his persistence he will get up and give him as much as he needs" (Luke 11:5-8).

Jesus told this parable on an occasion when He was talking to His disciples about prayer. (We will come back to that in a bit.) So it is right to understand this parable as calling His hearers' attention to something about what prayer is like.

What is the point to this simple story? The answer to that question must come from what is being emphasized. For most readers of this parable, the answer is something like, "Jesus wants His followers to be persistent in prayer." That idea does seem to flow from Jesus' seemingly plain statement: "I tell you, even though he will not get up and give him anything because he is his friend, yet *because of his persistence* he will get up and give him as much as he needs" (emphasis mine). That is hard to miss. Persistence does seem to be at the heart of this parable.

IF YOU REALLY WANT SOMETHING

As I take that simple idea (drawn from this parable) to heart, it is easy for me to conclude that the reason I do not get my prayers answered (in the affirmative) is that I, somehow, lack persistence. Perhaps you have also had those moments—or heard comments from some well-meaning friend—that "if only you had kept praying . . . " or "if you just keep believing . . . "

It is almost as if we think God is a reluctant Dispenser of blessings and grace; and by our badgering Him—like small children who incessantly beg for the parents to give them specific things—He will, somewhat begrudgingly, grant our requests. We wear Him down by our persistence; and in the end, He gives in—as long as we do not give up in the asking.

Knowing what we do about God and His desires to do good to His children[32] and to respond to those who come to Him in time of need[33], we should not think that this parable is intended to portray God as reluctant to respond to prayer, bothered by those who pray, or too preoccupied with other things to attend to a request for help. Such a view of God seems totally inconsistent with what Jesus teaches about what the Father is like. Although persistence matters, it cannot be about wearing God down until He gives us what we insist on.

So if persistence is not about winning God over through our incessant pleading, why else might Jesus encourage persistence in prayer? As I listen to this parable and feel Jesus' prod to think about my own praying, a few thoughts about persistence (or my lack of persistence) come into view.

If you were to listen in on my praying, I think you would see that I am often not very persistent. Sure, in the moment when the need is first and foremost in my thinking, I might pray fervently for a time. But my stick-to-itiveness does not take long to wane. My praying thins out, becomes tepid, not so urgent, lacking intensity. There are a few things that appear to contribute to this waning in my prayer life.

As I press on in prayer, talking to the Lord about some particular situation, I can find myself multi-tasking. What I mean is that while I am asking Him to do something about a specific need, I find myself simultaneously thinking through alternatives as to how I might address the need I have brought before Him on my own.

Sure, I do talk with Him about what seems so pressing, but I do not put all my eggs in that one basket. I am considering my options.

Maybe Jesus' picture of persistence is a call to abandon all other options, to come before God in prayer in such a way that we are not hedging our bets and entertaining other solutions if God does not come through. Maybe persistence in prayer is less about getting God to give in to our appeal and more about getting us to be "all in," looking only to God for a solution.

I recognize that there might be another factor that undermines my persistence in prayer. It is another dimension to that sense of desperateness when facing some need or some situation. Alongside my entertaining alternative solutions, sometimes, my prayer wanes because I just decide I can do without any answer, any solution. I may pray for a while—measured in days at times and measured in minutes most of the time—but then I begin to be distracted by other needs and concerns and issues and settle into thinking I can get by if nothing really ever happens regarding a matter in which I was, for a moment, fervent in prayer. Rather than lacking the desperation for God alone to answer the need, I end up lacking any real sense that the need must be addressed at all.

Maybe Jesus' picture of persistence is a call to be more honest about how desperate the situations we face really are, to come before God in prayer in such a way that we deeply feel that something *must* be done about this need or life will be drastically altered—and not for the better. Maybe persistence in prayer is less about a once-and-done approach to request making and more about a realization that we are facing something that must change.

BUT WHAT DO YOU REALLY WANT?

These two lacks—no desperation for God alone to bring a solution and no desperation that something must be done about the situation—tend to be what dampen the fires of my persistence in prayer. Recognizing that is helpful, but recognizing it still does not appear to be what is at is the heart of this parable.

Look back. Notice how prayer is pictured: "Friend, lend me three loaves; for a friend of mine has come to me from a journey, and I have nothing to set before him." Notice the request. The request—what is pictured about prayer—is not a persistent asking for personal need but a desperate cry for provision for the need of another.

Without reducing this parable to an allegory, we still must see that the one asking with persistence is not asking, fundamentally, for his personal needs. Yes, in the parable, the one asking has a lack. But in the parable, what prompts the asking is the need that has arisen because of the presence (and need) of another. This parable is not so much a picture of intensive and extensive prayer to get what I need but a call to persistent asking on behalf of the needs of another.

What is so sad about the way we often read this parable—and much of Jesus' teaching about prayer—is that we focus on how we can get things from God for ourselves. We make prayer almost exclusively about what I feel I need for myself. (And, by the way, we may feel that we are like nagging children in our praying because we recognize, but do not want to admit, that most of our praying is self-focused.) But here, persistent prayer is pictured as the way we can partner with God to see His resources brought to bear on the needs of others.

If we are attentive to the context of this parable, we might just see this idea of prayer as a means of bringing God's resources into the lives of others. Let's look back at the setting for this little story.

> It happened that while Jesus was praying in a certain place, after He had finished, one of His disciples said to Him, "Lord, teach us to pray just as John also taught his disciples." And He said to them, "When you pray, say: 'Father, hallowed be Your name. Your kingdom come. Give us each day our daily bread. And forgive us our sins, for we ourselves also forgive everyone who is indebted to us. And lead us not into temptation'" (Luke 11:1-4).

It was the disciples' request for Jesus to teach them to pray that gave rise to these words and the parable that immediately follows. Attentiveness to these few verses may well provide helpful insight into the right way to understand the parable.

The disciples' question is simple (but sometimes misread). They want Jesus to teach them to pray. But not just any way—they do not want Him to give them words merely to repeat. When they ask Jesus to teach them to pray "just as John also taught his disciples," they are asking for something in particular.

John taught his followers to pray the way he prayed. That is, John helped his disciples understand not just what he said when he prayed (as if John had some magic words that made prayer effective) but to help them learn to pray the way John himself prayed. By asking the question the way they did, Jesus' disciples wanted the same kind of thing. They wanted to learn from Jesus not what words to repeat but how to pray the way that Jesus Himself prayed. Over their time with Him, they had seen something different in Jesus' life of prayer; and they wanted to learn about that.

Without unpacking all there is to be discovered in this sample prayer,[34] there is something to be noted that will underscore for us the intent of the parable that follows. Although so many of us who have learned "the Lord's prayer" use it as a model for praying for ourselves and for our own personal needs, that is not what is in view.

After the first phrases in the prayer that invite the person praying to ask for God's will and His kingdom to be established, Jesus could have said, "Give *me* this day *my* daily bread." But He did not. The pronouns are all plural—the prayer is not a model of merely making requests for what you might personally need (although such praying does have a place in the Christian life— the Psalms are filled with examples of people talking with the Lord about their personal concerns and needs) but a model of praying on behalf of others.

The only sincere way to pray "the Lord's prayer" is to be aware of and attentive to the needs of others. That, of course, makes so much sense if we realize that Jesus is teaching His followers to pray the way that He Himself prayed. Jesus was not self-consumed; He walked among us as a servant, giving His life for the good of others.[35] And if that is the way He lived, that is certainly the way He prayed.

FROM A DIFFERENT PERSPECTIVE

Once we notice the setting in which Jesus tells this parable, we might listen to the parable from a different perspective. Rather than thinking that Jesus is calling His followers—and us—to be persistent in asking the Father for what we personally need, we might begin to see this parable as an elaboration and exposition of the other-centered character of "the Lord's prayer." It is the chips and salsa that fits with the Mexican meal. It is the bread and olive oil that goes with good Italian fare.

Seeing as Jesus modeled and taught His followers to pray for "us"—to have others in view in our praying—the parable underscores how we participate in prayer for others: through persistence with the expectation that God intends to bestow His resources for others through our praying.

Any journey through the Gospels will give us glimpses into Jesus' prayer life. Although we are not often told the specifics of His praying, we see Him going off alone to pray,[36] notice how He was praying when He was baptized,[37] and watch as He prays on the Mount of Transfiguration.[38]

When Jesus is in the Garden of Gethsemane, awaiting His betrayal at the hands of Judas, we do get to listen in on His prayers.[39] Although we will not unpack what can be discovered in Jesus' prayer recorded for us there, we must note that He does, in fact, pray for Himself. Minimally, we can recognize that even Jesus knew there were times to pray for one's own personal needs.

However, when Jesus was explaining about how His followers were to live, He called them (and us) to pray for our enemies, to pray for those who mistreat or persecute us.[40] It is provocative to see that Jesus does not call His followers to pray for themselves when facing hardship at the hands of others; He calls them to pray for those who are doing them harm. It is a prayer for others, not for themselves. And there are other snapshots of Jesus' prayers that help provide us a richer portrait of His prayer life.

Shortly before Jesus' betrayal, anticipating what was to come, Jesus explained to Simon Peter that Satan intended to "sift" His disciples. Jesus went on to underscore that, in the face of that coming trouble, He had prayed for Peter: "'Simon, Simon, behold, Satan has demanded *permission* to sift you like wheat; but I have prayed for you, that your faith may not fail; and you, when once you have turned again, strengthen your brothers'" (Luke 22:31-32).

Even though Jesus was Himself facing His greatest challenge, His praying had others in mind. Like the parable we have been looking at, Jesus is the "friend in the middle," praying for God's resources to be experienced in the life of another.

We could also turn to the longest prayer of Jesus recorded for us in the Gospels. It is found in John 17, where we listen in as Jesus is praying on the evening He was betrayed, gathered with His followers. (It would be good for you to read that prayer before proceeding with this chapter. It is a bit too long to put, in its entirety, in this book.)

Some of Jesus' praying in that chapter does have His own life and ministry in mind. He asks the Father to glorify Him (17:1). He prays for a restoration of His full experience of intimacy with the Father (17:5). But even in those requests, Jesus has in mind the benefit that would accrue to His followers in making those petitions (17:2, 3-4). What is clear is that Jesus is praying for others, even at this climactic moment of ministry. Specifically, He raises His voice and says:

- "I ask on their behalf; I do not ask on behalf of the world, but of those whom You have given Me" (17:9).
- "They themselves are in the world, and I come to you. Holy Father, keep them in Your name" (17:11).
- "I do not ask You to take them out of the world, but to keep them from the evil *one*" (17:15).
- "Sanctify them in the truth" (17:17).
- "I do not ask on behalf of these alone, but for those also who believe in Me through their word; that they may all be one; even as You, Father, *are* in Me and I in You, that they also may be in Us, so that the world may believe that You sent Me" (17:20-21).

As we listen in on Jesus' prayer, He is asking the Father for what His followers need. He is praying for others. He is standing as the friend in the middle. His intentional focus in prayer is on what would benefit others.

Some years ago, there was a fad that moved through the Christian world: WWJD? That acronym stood for "What Would Jesus Do?" It was intended to be a nudge to stir thinking about how Jesus would act in a particular situation.

Jesus' disciples were asking a slightly different question: HWJP? How Would Jesus Pray? The focus was not merely on the words Jesus used in prayer. They wanted more. They wanted to understand how Jesus prayed. And He told them. He gave them some guidelines in the Lord's Prayer. And then Jesus gave them the parable we have been looking at—a parable that pictures prayer as persistence, but not just about persistence. It is a parable about being persistent in asking for the needs of others.

It is not wrong to take our own needs to the Lord in prayer; there is a place for that. But if we want to grow in our lives in prayer—grow up to pray the way Jesus prays—the perspective may need to change. Prayer could become the means by which we participate with God in seeing His resources brought to bear on the needs of others. Prayer could actually reflect more of the character and ministry of Jesus.

REFLECTING ON THIS TRUTH
FOR PERSONAL REFLECTION:

1. No one would deny that the Bible clearly invites us to make our personal requests known to God. We are freely invited to ask Him for what we need. That is a part of the life of prayer. But even knowing that, we might be forced to wrestle with questions about our prayer life. How much of my praying is only about me, about what touches my life, about my needs?

2. The "Lord's Prayer" is so well-known, you have likely prayed that prayer before. Think back about how you have thought about that prayer. When you voiced those words, were you primarily thinking about yourself or about others? Were you praying an "us" kind of prayer or a "me" kind of prayer? How does this

parable we have looked at inform the way we should understand that model for prayer?

3.   Perhaps you have never thought much about Jesus' life of prayer. After all, there are not a huge number of texts that touch on it. But we do learn a great deal about Jesus' character and concern for others as we travel with Him in the Gospels. Does the One we meet in the Gospels strike you as a self-concerned individual? Seeing as He gives His life away for the good of others, what implications would arise from that about the focus of His praying?

FOR GROUP DISCUSSION:

1.   What kind of shift in thinking had to happen in your understanding of this parable to realize it might be more about persistence in praying for others than merely persistent in talking to God about your own needs?

2.   What kinds of things keep you from being persistent in praying for the needs of others? Why do we tend to tell others we will pray for them when they share a concern but then fall short in persistent praying on their behalf?

3.   How does this picture of persistent praying fit better with what you know to be true about the way Jesus Himself lived?

CHAPTER FIVE

MORE THAN MORE

THE MAN WITH THE PRODUCTIVE FARM

"And I will say to my soul, '. . . Take your ease . . . and be merry.'"

Luke 12:16

I REMEMBER A STORY I came across many years ago. It was an account of a missionary at work among an unreached people group. He labored for a long time to provide the Scriptures in the language of the people he was seeking to reach. And once the translation was available, he began to teach them the Gospel and teach them to read. God's grace reached this people group, and a number of them came to find life in Jesus.

As the little community of faith grew, the missionary began to invest in a few of the men with the hope of raising up some elders. He would sit with them around a table, the open Bible in front of them. These men grew as he read and taught them, sharing the copy of the Bible, as that was all they originally had.

After some time, the missionary was called away. He left the growing congregation (and the Bible he had translated) in the hands of the men he had trained, hoping one day to return and continue his labor of love among them. Ultimately, he was able to return and happily sat again with the men in whom he had invested so much time. He asked them about the church. He asked them how they were growing in faith in Jesus. And he asked them to share with him what they were learning from the Scriptures.

You can imagine his surprise when the men took turns reading a passage of Scripture and explaining what they read by taking hold of the Bible and turning it upside down or sideways. Although one of the men held the book before him in the expected way, another turned it completely upside down before reading. One turned the book ninety degrees to the right before reading, another ninety degrees to the left. Then it dawned on the missionary. They were reading the Bible the way they had learned.

Reflecting on those early days with these one-day-elders as they sat around the table with the open Bible as he read and explained the Scriptures to them, the missionary realized one typically saw the book upside down. Another saw the book from the right, while another from the left. Apparently, each ended up assuming that the way they saw the book from where they sat when they first learned to read was the way to read. They learned to read from a certain perspective; and each then continued to read, with the book open, from the original vantage point they had when they first learned to read.

You might think this a fanciful tale, accustomed as we are reading text from left to right, from the top of the page down the page line by line. But Hebrew is not read that way—Hebrew is read right to left. Some oriental languages are read top to bottom, the lines of text going down the page rather than across the page. So it might be possible for someone to learn to read the Bible very differently than we typically do. And that is the point.

Although we (that is, English Bible readers) all read the text on the page left to right, top to bottom, we all still read from a particular vantage point. We read texts from the perspective we had from our earliest days of learning to read Scripture. All too often, we can come to a passage with some assumed familiarity about what the passage is all about and end up reading with our conclusion firmly in mind, inhibiting us from actually engaging with the text.

Our perspectival reading of text is not about turning the page one way or another but about turning the meaning of the text one way or another to make it fit what we are accustomed to thinking about the Gospel, about Jesus, about life with Him, about Scripture. This is not to suggest we intentionally misread texts but only to recognize that every time we open the book, we begin with a tendency to read it from our preferred vantage point. Sometimes, that is not all that troubling, but there are times that our perspective obscures what the passage we are reading actually means.

So what is the solution? What can we do about this tendency? Simply put, we need to try to read every passage we come to with a tenacious desire to hear what the author is saying. We need to privilege the voice of the Spirit-inspired author and listen attentively. We need to hold our personal biases loosely and pursue all and only what is there in the text before us.

The parable in view in this chapter may seem, on first read, to be fairly straightforward and clear. (But caution is needed! Do not simply read the text from your favored vantage point.) In fact, it appears that Jesus Himself made a fairly clear application of the parable.

> And [Jesus] told them a parable, saying, "The land of a rich man was very productive. And he began reasoning to himself, saying, 'What shall I do, since I have no place to store my crops?' Then he said, 'This is what I will do: I will tear down my barns and build larger ones, and there I will store all my grain and my goods. 'And I will say to my soul, "Soul, you have many goods laid up for many years *to come*; take your ease, eat, drink *and* be merry."' But God said to him, 'You fool! This *very* night your soul is required of you; and *now* who will own what you have prepared?' So is the man who stores up treasure for himself, and is not rich toward God" (Luke 12:16-21).

Like with all parables, we need to be attentive to the simple "punch line" of the story. What is quite striking about this parable is that there is nothing in the story that indicates anything necessarily blameworthy in the actions of the rich man—but he is nevertheless identified as a fool.

The man had a very productive field. He did not want to let the crops go to waste or rot, so he appears to take a reasonable step— he will find a way to preserve the bounty. Even his assessment that he now had sufficient stored for many years may not be at all blameworthy.[41] After all, this is what Joseph did when he was in

Egypt—he stored up the bounty of seven fruitful years in order to ensure provision for seven lean years to come (Gen. 41).

The climax of the parable comes when God "requires"[42] the rich man's soul. And the question asked is critical: "Who will own what you have prepared?" This, apparently, is what is foolish.[43] And Jesus explained: "So is the man who stores up treasure for himself, and is not rich toward God." Clearly, the parable is intended to picture foolish living—and the contrast pictured is between being "rich" and being "rich toward God."

Is it just that the man had much? Is it that he stored up so much? Is it that he thought he had provision for the future? Apparently the "storing up treasure" is problematic. But how does one become "rich toward God"? What would it mean to store up treasures with respect to God?

There is a word in the question asked of the rich man that can help us home in on what is essential in understanding this parable. The question asked of the man is, "Who will own what you have *prepared*?" That word helps us clarify the man's foolishness. Although a parable is not an account of something that actually happened, it still is worth asking: in the story, what was the man preparing for?

As we wrestle with the implications of this parable, it is helpful to look back at what prompted Jesus' story—seeing the reason for the parable may help us understand the point.

> Someone in the crowd said to Him, "Teacher, tell my brother to divide the *family* inheritance with me." But He said to him, "Man, who appointed Me a judge or arbitrator over you?" Then He said to them, "Beware,

and be on your guard against every form of greed; for not *even* when one has an abundance does his life consist of his possessions." And He told them a parable, saying . . . (Luke 12:13-16).

What did the man in the crowd want? Apparently, his father had died; and his brother (likely his elder brother, the executor of the estate) had not distributed the inheritance—something the man expected as rightly his own. So seeing that Jesus was wise, the man asked Him to help. But why did Jesus respond as He did?

It is not immediately obvious from the text exactly what Jesus intended in saying what He did. It would be inconsistent with Jesus' character for us to conclude He was being dismissive or rude. It is likely He intended to provoke the man to think about what he was asking. What might Jesus have wanted? How could the question that Jesus asked be answered?

To answer that question, the man would have had to reflect on why he thought Jesus was the One to rightly assess the situation he was facing. But Jesus held no judicial role in the community— He was not a judge or an officially appointed arbitrator. Perhaps all that Jesus was pressing on was for the man (and those listening) to recognize that Jesus did have some authority—perhaps God-granted—to speak to life issues. If that was the case, what Jesus said next carried much greater weight. It was not just the opinion of a nice teacher, but an authoritative word.

Jesus did not say that the man was wrong in wanting the inheritance to be rightly divided. But He did raise a word of caution. He spoke about greed. He spoke about the pursuit of getting or having more. And what is the ground for this caution? "For not even when one has an abundance does his life consist of his possessions."

What did Jesus mean in referring to "an abundance"? Earlier in Luke, that word was used to refer to what the disciples picked up after the multitude was fed (9:12-17). They gathered up the broken pieces that were "left over." The abundance was not some opulent, over-the-top excess—it was just more than was needed at the moment. Everyone—including the disciples—had eaten and were satisfied; and then there were the baskets left over. So Jesus' warning was not a blanket ban on having stuff. He was cautioning the man who asked the question—and all those who were listening—not to think that the stuff one has defines one's life.

ASSEMBLING THE PIECES

We now may have enough pieces on the table to assemble the puzzle of what is going on in this parable. The man whose request launched this parable only wanted Jesus to help him obtain what he thought was rightfully his own. And Jesus did not tell the man his desire was wicked. Jesus only raised the caution that more stuff does not mean one will enjoy more life.

This is followed by the parable. And what is pictured in that story is a man who ended up with more stuff—but who is identified as a fool. Jesus clarified what He was driving at by contrasting a person who stores up treasure for himself and is not "rich toward God." Neither in addressing the man's question nor in telling the parable did Jesus simply condemn having stuff or praise the idea of owning nothing. Jesus did not imply or suggest that the man looking for his inheritance (or the man in the parable) was damned, cut off from God, or wicked. Jesus raised a caution about being a fool.

In the New Testament, there are two words that are translated "fool."[44] Although they are similar in meaning, there seems to be a shade of difference in what these words convey. The word Jesus used here conveys the idea of an almost laughable inattentiveness to what should be obvious. It is as if He is asking, "Did you not recognize something so obvious?"

Only one other time in Luke do we find Jesus using this word:

> Now when He had spoken, a Pharisee asked Him to have lunch with him; and He went in, and reclined *at the table*. When the Pharisee saw it, he was surprised that He had not first ceremonially washed before the meal. But the Lord said to him, "Now you Pharisees clean the outside of the cup and of the platter; but inside of you, you are full of robbery and wickedness. You foolish ones, did not He who made the outside make the inside also?" (Luke 11:37-40).

There are times when Jesus had a sterner word for the Pharisees.[45] But here the remark is a bit gentler. I can see Jesus smiling as He points out the seeming ludicrous nature of thinking that merely outward cleaning would really get at the heart of the problem (no pun intended). That would be like simply washing the outside of a cup before using it without bothering to clean the inside—where the coffee had been sitting for a few days and had started to show evidence of moldy contamination!

Let's go back to our parable, armed with an understanding of the word Jesus used. The man in the parable was foolish—it was almost laughable to store up a bunch of goods without any regard for why and for whom he was stocking the goods away. That parable was prompted by the question about dividing an inheritance. Jesus' reply should have nudged the man making the request to think, "Why am I doing this?" That seems to be the point of question asked of the man in the parable: "Who will own what you have prepared?"

Once we see why Jesus offered this parable and begin to grasp the punch line of the parable, we are brought face to face with the issue Jesus is addressing. Maybe it is not so much about the stuff—Jesus is not condemning having goods. Maybe it is more about having the right perspective. Maybe foolishness is all about the *why* and not so much about the *what*.

When this parable is read as if it is simply about having too much stuff or about how we should give away stuff—when the point is made about the stuff—then we can actually insulate ourselves from what Jesus is saying. We can start doing some financial accounting. How much is in the bank account? How does our house or lifestyle compare to others around us? Are we "middle class"? Or are we more than that—or less than that? What is the right percentage to give? Is a "tenth" enough?

As we have noted, Jesus did not condemn the man who wanted his fair share of the inheritance, nor did Jesus' parable picture the man who had experienced a bountiful windfall as wicked. Although the presenting issue in this account is material stuff, beneath that is the thing that is of primary concern. The main question really seems to be, why are you living the way you are living? What are you living for? Those questions need to be answered in light of this parable.

In writing to his apprentice, Timothy, Paul underscored a similar idea. In his first letter, the apostle wrote, "Instruct those who are rich in this present world not to be conceited or to fix their hope on the uncertainty of riches, but on God, who richly supplies us with all things to enjoy. *Instruct them* to do good, to be rich in good works, to be generous and ready to share . . . so that they may take hold of that which is life indeed" (1 Tim. 6:17-19).

It is important to note that Paul is not dismissive about those who are rich;[46] apparently, to have much stuff is not necessarily a problem. It is not the stuff you have that is as big a concern as how you are thinking about life in light of the stuff you have.

What is a spiritually healthy attitude in the face of having stuff? Someone who has much must think well about the stuff. A rich person is not to be conceited—not "high-minded," holding a view of himself where he sees himself living above others in their world. Even with an abundance, those who are rich are to have their confidence about the future anchored in God Himself, not in what they have in the bank. After all, Paul says that stuff is "uncertain"; not only is wealth variable, but Paul's language suggests that in and of itself, wealth is pointless.

Seeing as God provides His own with all things to enjoy (our God is not stingy in the bestowal of His blessings), all people—even the rich—can rightly enjoy God's graciousness. But such enjoyment is not the proper end point for daily living. Real riches are found in living the life God intends for His people—and that would mean being rich (abundant!) in good works. The stuff we might enjoy is not merely for our own enjoyment—it is not to be spent merely on ourselves (as apparently was the case with the man pictured in the parable). Generosity and a willingness—an eagerness—to share with others brings into focus the heart of the issue.

We have to ask ourselves, "Why I am living with 'stuff' the way I am? What am I living for in the enjoyment of God's rich provisions for me? What good things does God have planned for the stuff He has placed in my hands?" Only then will we be living into the life that is truly life—the life that God richly provides for all His children.

REFLECTING ON THIS TRUTH
FOR PERSONAL REFLECTION:

1. One cannot make the case from Scripture that material blessings, in and of themselves, are wicked. After all, more than once, God blessed those who walked with Him with riches. But that should not keep us from thinking well about "stuff." So when you think about your stuff—your possessions, your bank account, the money in your pocket—how do you think about it? Do you see it as something you have earned or deserved? What might change if you began to think that the stuff that the Lord has entrusted to you is

so you can joyously participate with Him in living in open-handed generosity?

2. That first-blush reading of this parable—with the conclusion that there was something wrong with the man having much—leads to an attitude of simply managing our possessions. How does the understanding unpacked in this chapter provoke you to think differently about what you have? How does the challenge to wrestle with *why* you have what you do and *why* you gather what you do press on you differently than just hoping you are managing your stuff well?

3. If we see Paul's words to Timothy as something of a commentary on the parable, what does Paul add to our thinking about possessions? How do his words enrich or deepen your understanding of the right way to think about what God has given you and how God has blessed you materially?

FOR GROUP DISCUSSION:

1. Can you see yourself in the position of the man who asked Jesus about the dividing of His inheritance? What would have been behind his question? Can you identify with his desire for what would seem to be fair?

2. What help is it, in coming to understand this parable, to see what prompted the parable? How does the

man's question about having the inheritance divided set the framework for the parable?

3. How does the parable's impact reach you when you understand that Jesus' point is less about the stuff you have and more about how you think about the stuff you have? That it is less about what you have and more about why you have what you do?

CHAPTER SIX

WHAT ARE WE WAITING FOR?

THE FAITHFUL AND SENSIBLE STEWARD

"'Who then is the faithful and sensible steward,
whom his master will put in charge of his servants?'"

Luke 12:42

I LOVE A GOOD DETECTIVE story. I am a fan of Arthur Conan Doyle's classic Sherlock Holmes tales. I have read a lot of other mysteries over the years and have come to conclude that there is a rather simple way to distinguish a good detective story from a mediocre or even poor mystery.

When you arrive at the end of a good detective story, you realize that the clues have been there all along. The world-famous detective—whether Sherlock Holmes or Hercule Poirot or Miss Marple or Nancy Drew or Father Brown—recognized the clues that were there in the story and put them together in a reasonable, albeit startling, way. And thus, the mystery is solved. The less-than-good mystery story leaves you with the clear sense that the brilliant detective had access to information or insight that you, as the reader, did not have. The mystery may have been solved, but you are left saying, "What? The murdered person was a twin? How did the detective get his hands on the secret will? Why did the author not tell us that the house was built on an abandoned bomb shelter? Who knew there was a secret passage in the house?"

It feels unfair for the detective to have access to facts that we, as readers, do not have and for them to know things that we, as readers, are not privy to. We feel cheated out of a good story. After all, there is no way for us to have solved the crime because there was information we did not know.

As unfair as that feels when we read a fictional detective story, there is a similar unfairness in the way we sometimes read Gospel narratives. Seeing as we know much more about the end of the story than those we encounter in the Gospel accounts, we can read our understanding into passages when those in the account could not know what we know. It is not a matter of pretending we do not know what we do (from other places in the New Testament), but it is a matter of reading the narrative honestly. To read honestly means to read to discover what the author intended his original readers to grasp. If we do not refrain from reading what we know into the account of people growing in their understanding of Jesus and His teachings (as we find it in the Gospels), we will invariably misconstrue what we find in those narratives.

We are not dealing with fictional stories when we read the Gospels. It will not do to think that all that matters is that we have the "big story" of the Gospels in mind when we read.[47] We need to read and listen with an awareness of what those in the narrative would have known if we want to faithfully understand the texts we are reading.

IT HAPPENED INCREMENTALLY

Jesus did have a cohesive, coherent, and clear message to declare. He announced the kingdom's presence and spoke of His own work as the carrying out of the Father's plan.[48] But He did not back up the theological truck and dump out all that was included in His message at one time. He presented the message incrementally. He was not vague or elusive; but He did take His time, teaching what He wanted His disciples to know in a step-by-step way.[49]

The implications of this are clear. When we read the Gospels and listen to what Jesus says to those He is with, we need to understand His words with the understanding they would have had. We need to listen incrementally.

Turning to the parable in view in this chapter, we will need to put this approach into practice. We start with a couple of short parables, and then we turn our attention to a longer—and, perhaps, misunderstood—parable.

Jesus' ministry had been growing. Luke reports that so many thousands of people were gathering around Him that they were stepping on one another (Luke 12:1). In the midst of that crowd, Jesus addressed those who were intent on following Him (His disciples) calling them to not worry about their lives, for the Father cared for them (12:2-12).

Someone in the larger crowd cried out to Jesus, asking Him to resolve an inheritance issue, and Jesus cautioned that man (and the crowd) against all kinds of greediness (12:13-21). Jesus underscored the need to be "rich toward God" (12:21)—to find one's treasure in God Himself. Jesus is not talking about doing a lot of good things to earn a place "in heaven," but living as if God Himself was what was most to be valued. Having said that, Jesus again turned His attention away from the larger crowd that was gathered and addressed His disciples (12: 22-34). He spoke to them with great clarity: "'And do not seek what you will eat and what you will drink, and do not keep worrying. For all these things the nations of the world eagerly seek; but your Father knows that you need these things. But seek His kingdom, and these things will be added to you. Do not be afraid, little flock, for your Father has chosen gladly to give you the kingdom'" (Luke 12:29-32).

Here is the first place that we need to be attentive to what Jesus is saying and what it would have meant to those who were listening to Him at that moment. What is it that we need to notice to think well about what He said? We need to understand the reference to "the kingdom."

IT WASN'T THE FIRST TIME

We do not have to go back very far in Luke's account to get a broader context for understanding what Jesus was talking about in referring to "the kingdom":

- "But He said to them, "I must preach the kingdom of God to the other cities also, for I was sent for this purpose"" (Luke 4:43).
- "Soon afterwards, He *began* going around from one city and village to another, proclaiming[50] and preaching the kingdom of God" (Luke 8:1).
- "And He sent [the twelve] out to proclaim the kingdom of God and to perform healing" (Luke 9:2).
- "But the crowds . . . followed Him; and welcoming them, He *began* speaking to them about the kingdom of God and curing those who had need of healing" (Luke 9:11).
- In sending out seventy disciples to extend His ministry, Jesus said, "'Heal those . . . who are sick, and say to them, "The kingdom of God has come near to you"''" (Luke 10:9).
- "'But if I cast out demons by the finger of God, then the kingdom of God has come upon you'" (Luke 11:20).

These passages are the background for how the disciples would have understood Jesus' words about seeking the kingdom. What He said makes it clear that Jesus was not primarily referring to some far off and distant future kingdom. His language about proclaiming the kingdom and the kingdom being at hand[51] make no sense if we (mistakenly) think He is talking about Heaven far off and distant in both time and space.

So, in Luke 12:29-32, when He called His disciples to seek the kingdom and encouraged them by explaining the Father "has chosen to freely give you the kingdom," Jesus was speaking about a present experience of the breaking in of God's kingdom. That present experience of the kingdom breaking in—announced and mediated by Jesus and extended through both the twelve and the seventy—is the framework for the picture that is presented in the parables that follow.

> "Be dressed in readiness, and *keep* your lamps lit. Be like men who are waiting for their master when he returns from the wedding feast, so that they may immediately open *the door* to him when he comes and knocks. Blessed are those slaves whom the master will find on the alert when he comes; truly I say to you, that he will gird himself *to serve,* and have them recline *at the table,* and will come up and wait on them. Whether he comes in the second watch, or even in the third, and finds *them* so, blessed are those *slaves.* But be sure of this, that if the head of the house had known at what hour the thief was coming, he would not have allowed his house to be broken into. You too, be ready; for the Son of Man is coming at an hour that you do not expect" (Luke 12:35-40).

The emphasis in these two short parables is clear: to be ready and alert. The reason for this attentiveness: "For the Son of Man is coming at an hour that you do not expect."

But we have to ask what those listening to Him would have been thinking as they heard these words. What would they have understood by Jesus' reference to the coming of the Son of Man? Although there is no specific mention of the kingdom in these parables, how we think about that idea does have bearing on how we read and hear these words. If we are thinking of the kingdom as some far off and distant future event or place, then we are going to read the reference to the "coming of the Son of Man" in a particular way. But if we are thinking about the kingdom as a present reality in the same way as those who were listening to these words as Jesus spoke them, we might think about the Son of Man's coming in a fresh way—and, perhaps, more in line with what Jesus truly meant.

Prior to this moment, Jesus has only spoken a few times of the coming of the Son of Man. He has referred to Himself as the Son of Man in speaking of His ministry (Luke 5:24; 6:5). Although His disciples did not fully understand what He meant at the moment, Jesus also spoke of the Son of Man suffering and dying and being raised (9:22, 44). But before this reference at the end of these two short parables, Jesus only made two specific comments about the "coming of the Son of Man:"

- "The Son of Man has come eating and drinking, and you say, 'Behold, a gluttonous man and a drunkard, a friend of tax collectors and sinners!'" (Luke 7:34)
- "For whoever is ashamed of Me and My words, the Son of Man will be ashamed of him when He comes in His glory, and *the glory* of the Father and of the holy angels" (Luke 9:26).

It is clear that in the first of these references Jesus is speaking of His active, present ministry. Speaking of the coming of the

Son of Man, He is talking about what He is actually doing. He is present; He has come; He is working.

The second reference is more provocative. Jesus referred to the Son of Man coming in glory. What is challenging about what He said here is that He did not unpack what that "coming in glory" referred to. Minimally, those who heard these words would have had to think of some yet-to-be-seen glory in the near future and not necessarily about a far off and distant future event.

But could they have understood these words as referring to a post-death, post-resurrection, post-ascension, thousands-of-years-in-the-future return of the ascended Christ to the earth to establish His earthly rule? That seems quite unlikely. Jesus had not told them enough about what was to come in the distant future for them to have thought such things. We might understand some (or more) of the implications of Jesus' statement recorded in Luke 9. Nevertheless, it would be unreasonable to conclude His hearers' thinking was shaped by what we know but what they could not have known.

How might his original hearers have understood the two short parables we looked at in Luke 12:35-40? If we do not read our sense of Jesus' second coming into the parables, what is the point of the stories? The parables are about attentiveness to the arrival—either of the master (who, interestingly enough, will serve his servants) or the robber. These seem like radically different images, but the idea is the same in each: to be alert and attentive so as not to miss what could happen at any moment.

At the close of Jesus' exchange with the crowds who were listening at the time He told these two short parables, Jesus clarified what He intended His hearers to be attentive to:

And He was also saying to the crowds, "When you see a cloud rising in the west, immediately you say, 'A shower is coming,' and so it turns out. And when *you see* a south wind blowing, you say, 'It will be a hot day,' and it turns out *that way*. You hypocrites! You know how to analyze the appearance of the earth and the sky, but why do you not analyze this present time?" (Luke 12:54-56)

It would seem that the two short parables we have read about attentiveness might not be about looking to the second coming of the Son of Man but being aware and attentive to what is happening through the then present ministry of the Son of Man Who has already come. Not to be attentive would result in overlooking or missing out on what He was doing right there in their midst.

Having listened well to what Jesus had been saying (in those two short parables), Peter then asked a question. The call for attentiveness to the "coming of the Son of Man" prompted the exchange that followed. And Jesus' answer gives us another parable—the one that is the final focus of this chapter.

Peter said, "Lord, are You addressing this parable to us, or to everyone *else* as well?" And the Lord said, "Who then is the faithful and sensible steward, whom his master will put in charge of his servants, to give them their rations at the proper time? Blessed is that slave whom his master finds so doing when he comes. Truly I say to you that he will put him in charge of all his possessions. But if that slave says in his heart, 'My master will be a long time in coming,' and begins to beat the slaves, *both* men and women, and to eat and drink and get drunk; the master of that slave will come on a day when he does not expect *him* and at an hour he does not know, and will cut him in pieces, and assign him a place with the unbelievers. And that slave who knew his master's will and did not get ready or act in accord with his will, will receive many lashes, but the one who did not know *it*, and committed deeds worthy of a flogging, will receive but few. From everyone who has been given much, much will be required; and to whom they entrusted much, of him they will ask all the more" (Luke 12:41-48).

Many Bible teachers look at this parable along the lines of how they read the parables about attentiveness we touched on earlier. They see this parable about calling for faithfulness in view of the future return of Christ to the earth after His death, resurrection, and ascension.[52]

It should not be denied that this parable might have implications for the future Second Coming of Christ. However, given what we have already looked at regarding the ongoing discussion in this section, is it reasonable to think that is how Peter would have understood this parable? In fact, why would Peter have asked about whether the earlier two short parables were addressed to the crowd or to him if he did not have some sense that there were immediate implications for his life touched on in what Jesus had said?

The parable closes with Jesus' charge: "From everyone who has been given much, much will be required; and to whom they entrusted much, of him they will ask all the more." And earlier, as we noted, Jesus told His followers, "Your Father has chosen gladly to give you the kingdom."

The disciples have already been entrusted with a call to extend the kingdom's presence and power into the lives of others (Luke 9:1-6, 10:1-10). Jesus has charged them with pursuing that kingdom (12:31-32). And now comes a parable about a sensible steward who needs to be responsible with what has been entrusted to him and to not misuse the authority granted to him by his master.

Is it not more likely that Peter and the others would be thinking more of what is going on, right there and then in their lives, rather than trying to figure out how things will play out at the end of time? Would that have not been the more pressing issue for them? And if that is the case—as it would seem—then we need to understand Peter's question and Jesus' reply in light of that.

As with all parables, the story is not true to life. As with many parables, the language is a bit hyperbolic in order to better drive home the point. As with every parable, the parable "lives" in a particular setting and is a reply to a specific issue at hand. In this setting, when Peter asked about whether the parables about attentiveness were addressed to everyone or just to the closer disciples, Jesus told a parable about those who are entrusted with a stewardship. Jesus turned from speaking to the crowd and was now addressing Peter and the closer band of disciples. Jesus answered Peter's question by providing a parable that pictured Peter and his companions' responsibility in light of the call to attentiveness. (And seeing as Jesus already called His followers to an ongoing participatory partnership with Him in ministry,[53] they must have had some sense of what their responsibility was to be—if they were only attentive.)

Despite the strong language Jesus used, I do not think this parable is about whether someone is saved or lost; I do not think Jesus is discussing issues of Heaven and Hell.[54] Attentive to the context in which this parable appears—Jesus speaking directly to His disciples whom He has already told that the Father has given them the kingdom (Luke 12:32)—it would be entirely out of place to now speak to them as if they were not yet participants in that kingdom.

Undoubtedly, in the broader context of this passage, it is critical to note that inattentiveness to what was happening in and through the ministry of Jesus will leave someone outside the kingdom. For Jesus' hearers, to not see and recognize the signs that are occurring all around them through Jesus' ministry will leave them on the outside looking in—they will be living like foolish hypocrites.[55]

WHAT ABOUT THE FIRST COMING?

As Jesus finished telling this parable, He did not stop speaking. What He went on to say can help us determine whether we are reading this parable appropriately.

> "I have come to cast fire upon the earth; and how I wish it were already kindled! But I have a baptism to undergo, and how distressed I am until it is accomplished! Do you suppose that I came to grant peace on earth? I tell you, no, but rather division; for from now on five *members*

in one household will be divided, three against two and two against three. They will be divided, father against son and son against father, mother against daughter and daughter against mother, mother-in-law against daughter-in-law and daughter-in-law against mother-in-law" (Luke 12:49-53).

Although Jesus did not use the "Son of Man" language here, it is impossible to miss the idea that He (the Son of Man) had already come, was present, and was at work. Although He had inaugurated His Father-given kingdom work, there was yet more to come; it was not yet fully accomplished. But the decisive nature of what He came to do was already underway. But some of Jesus' hearers had not noticed. Some of those in the crowds that were following Him were inattentive. Some lived as if the decisive nature of the kingdom of the Son of Man was still a long way off.

But Peter caught a glimpse of something. He realized that the call to attentiveness might well be addressed to him and others of Jesus' closest band of followers. So he asked for clarification. And Jesus responded with a parable. In one sense, we could say that Peter was already living in the implications of this parable; he was being attentive! That parable was not about what is yet far off and distant. The parable was not addressing where someone might or might not spend eternity. The parable underscored a profound and yet simple issue for the followers of Jesus.

What are you doing with what has been entrusted to you? Right now, today, given the present reality of the ongoing ministry of the Son of Man, Who has already come, how are you living? Having been granted participation in His kingdom, what are you doing with what has been entrusted to you? When we hear the parable Jesus spoke to Peter with this present-tense sense, we will not only understand it as having a greater impact on Peter and his companions, but it will also have a greater impact on us.

Too often, this parable of Jesus, in answer to Peter, is seen as a call to be "good stewards" as we live in the in-between time between Jesus' first coming and His second. But reading the parable that way leaves us to think like the slave in the parable who tells himself that his master "will be a long time in coming." We might convince ourselves that we are not anticipating a long delay in the return of Christ, but very few seem to live as if that return could be at any moment. To read the parable as referring to that future return may just leave us at risk of inattentiveness because we think that His return is not yet.

Hearing the present-tense sense of the parable—that Jesus was speaking of His presence, then and there, and that there was not a long waiting time for the manifestation of His kingdom—the call to daily attentiveness comes with fresh impact. Ever since Jesus' first coming, His followers must live in the reality that, at any moment, He might well be right there, in their midst. It is not an anticipation of a yet future arrival of the master but an awareness that the Master (although perhaps unnoticed in the moment) is ever-present. And, thus, we are awakened to the necessity of living in a daily awareness of His expectations for those who name Him as their Master.

REFLECTING ON THIS TRUTH

FOR PERSONAL REFLECTION:

1. Think back over the broader context in Luke 12 for understanding the presence of the kingdom. How have you tended to think of the kingdom? How does your view of the kingdom shape the way you have heard the parables touched on this chapter? How might the broader context in Luke of references to the kingdom challenge or shape your view?

2. When you come across the language of the "coming of the Son of Man" in the Gospels, how have you tended to understand that idea? Seeing as Jesus had not (at the point in time we encounter these parables) spoken to His followers of a future "second coming," why should we be cautious about reading that understanding in the parables touched on in this chapter? How might what we have been exploring shape the way you will think about the "coming of the Son of Man"?

3. When the parable that Jesus addressed to Peter in reply to his question is seen as having a more immediate present implication (instead of anticipating a long wait for the second coming), how does the impact of that parable change for you? What might end up being different in the way you think about today, let alone about your life, in the days to come?

FOR GROUP DISCUSSION:

1. In what ways could our perception of "kingdom" and "the coming of the Son of Man" lead us to misunderstandings about what Jesus said? How can we better hold loosely what we think we know when we come to any text?

2. Given that Jesus had already taught His followers about the presence of the kingdom and had previously spoken of His having come, how do you think His original hearers understood these two short parables?

3. Listening well to the exchange between Jesus and the crowd and Jesus and Peter, what is it that Jesus wanted for those who heard Him speak? What do you think Peter's concern was in asking what he did? What are the implications of Jesus' answer to Peter? And what bearing might that answer have on our lives?

CHAPTER SEVEN

WHEN THE SON
WENT ASTRAY

THE LOST SHEEP, THE LOST COIN, AND A LOST SON

"But we had to celebrate and rejoice."

Luke 15:32

YOU HAVE PROBABLY SEEN THE signs; they are quite common in growing suburban neighborhoods: "Drive like your kids live here." It is clever, catchy, and intended to alert drivers to be cautious about driving through the subdivision. And although the intent is clear, the wording is a bit misleading—if we stop long enough to pay attention to what the sign actually says.

In English, the word *like* only has a few basic grammatically acceptable usages[56]:

- It can mean "similar," as in "This burnt toast tastes *like* cardboard."

- It can mean "enjoy," as in "I actually *like* the taste of burnt toast."
- It can mean "want," as in "I would *like* some more burnt toast or some cardboard if you are out of toast."
- It can mean "choose," as in "You can have as much burnt toast as you *like*."
- It can mean "to do well in," as in "That houseplant seems to *like* burnt toast as a soil amendment."

Although it has become common usage, the way *like* is used on the sign is fundamentally a misuse. Only one of the possible usages would seem to fit the signage: Drive *similar* to the way your kids live. So does that mean I should drive compulsively, irresponsibly, enthusiastically, going until I fall asleep, or . . .

Of course, I am overstating to make a point. A misuse falls into common usage and is not only accepted but also broadly understood. All of this is in spite of the fact that the language itself does not mean what we think it means. That sometimes happens with parables. A misunderstanding of a parable falls into common usage, and the parable's meaning gets popularly hijacked. Because of how widely accepted the misunderstanding is, it becomes challenging for us to get at what Jesus was, in fact, saying. The "everyone thinks this way" approach to the neighborhood sign means we get it, even if the language is not quite right. But the "everyone thinks this way" approach to a parable might mean that we miss the real point because we have readily accepted common usage.

Before we turn to the particular parable in view, I recognize that I am not the only one seeking to read Jesus' parables well. I do not believe that my point of view is always (or even necessarily) exhaustively correct. What I do want to do is to approach every parable by attentively reading what is there in the passage. I want to let the setting and Jesus' words take precedent. I want to hold loosely my preconceived understandings of what this or that parable "must mean" (because of what I have always heard or because of what I have been told).

This approach comes with a few challenges. First, I find that I must read the Gospels with a more open, humble heart. I sincerely want to hear—as if for the first time—what Jesus is saying. Second, I have been finding this a bit harder than I initially anticipated. Because I am not defaulting to common usage, I am challenged to think hard and not read superficially. Lastly, I keep bumping up against commonly taught explanations of the parables—and those bumps often leave me on a different path to understanding what Jesus is saying.

Because my understanding of what Jesus is saying through this or that parable might differ from common (or even scholarly) opinion, it could seem that I am simply being contrarian or seeking to make some unique contribution. But that is never the case. Please keep that in mind as we read this very popular parable—known as the parable of the prodigal son. I may not end up where you have often been led when listening to an explanation of this parable. I do not understand this parable in the way it is commonly interpreted.

What does this mean for you, my reader? I have a few suggestions. Do not take my opinion as the final word or the only correct way to understand Jesus' parables. Do not assume that because I might end up at a different place than other teachers that I think their perspectives are wrong or valueless. Do join me in reading the passages in view with attentiveness and a prayer that the Spirit would help you (help us) to hear well what Jesus is saying. And, lastly, do what those who listened to the apostle Paul were commended for doing: search the Scriptures for yourself and become persuaded by what the texts themselves say (Acts 17:11).

DID YOU HEAR WHAT ELSE HE SAID?

So with that caveat, let us press on to the parable. The passage begins with this phrase: "And He said, 'A man had two sons'" (Luke 15:9). Did you notice it?

"*And* He said . . . "[57] That word means that the parable we are going to explore is attached to something; it follows a flow of thought. The "and" points back to something that preceded. If the "and He said" points us back to what came before, we can turn back a few verses. There, in Luke 15:8, we find, "Or what woman . . ." Again, that tells us that the parable that begins in 15:8 is building on something Jesus had already been explaining. If the "or what woman" points us back to what came before, we can turn back a few verses. There, in Luke 15:3, we read, "So He told them this parable, saying . . ." Again, the language tells us that we are in the flow of something Jesus was explaining; "*so* He told them" points us back to what prompted Jesus words—and why, ultimately, He told the parable of the prodigal son.

This means that for us to understand what Jesus is addressing in telling the parable about the son, we will have to go back to the beginning of Luke 15:

Now all the tax collectors and the sinners were coming near Him to listen to Him. Both the Pharisees and the scribes *began* to grumble, saying, "This man receives sinners and eats with them." So He told them this parable, saying, "What man among you, if he has a hundred sheep and has lost one of them, does not leave the ninety-nine in the open pasture and go after the one which is lost until he finds it? When he has found it, he lays it on his shoulders, rejoicing. And when he comes home, he calls together his friends and his neighbors, saying to them, 'Rejoice with me, for I have found my sheep which was lost!' I tell you that in the same way, there will be *more* joy in heaven over one sinner who repents than over ninety-nine righteous persons who need no repentance. Or what woman, if she has ten silver coins and loses one coin, does not light a lamp and sweep the house and search carefully until she finds it? When she has found it, she calls together her friends and neighbors, saying, 'Rejoice with me, for I have found the coin which I had lost!' In the same way, I tell you, there is joy in the presence of the angels of God over one sinner who repents" (Luke 15:1-10).

Jesus offers two short parables before we get to the parable of the prodigal in reply to an issue raised by some Pharisees and scribes. Their concern was that Jesus was eating with those who were—to their way of thinking—the undesirables. So what begins this series is a single concern: why do you, Jesus, hang out with the wrong people?

In response to this concern, Jesus tells the first short parable about a shepherd and some sheep. Remember that parables function in a way similar to a joke. This story is not an account of something that actually happened; the story contains elements that set things up for the punch line.

In the story of the shepherd and his sheep, Jesus is telling a story to make a point. No real shepherd would leave his sheep in the open pasture to go after one. If he did, he would likely come back to find his flock ravaged by wolves! That is part of the set up for the punch line.

What does the shepherd do when he finds the lamb he wanted? He rejoices and celebrates with his friends. It is right there that we touch on the point of the parable: When the shepherd finds what he wants, he rejoices. The shepherd sought out that lamb for joy!

In drawing this story to a close, Jesus explained, "I tell you that in the same way, there will be *more* joy in heaven over one sinner who repents than over ninety-nine righteous persons who need no repentance." But what is Jesus underscoring? Is Jesus making a point about repentance, or is He highlighting something about joy?

Think about this short parable. The actor in the parable is the shepherd. The lamb takes no action. The climax of the parable is the shepherd's joy. It is about his joy in finding what he wants. So Jesus' closing explanation—although mentioning repentance—underscores joy! When the shepherd finds what he wants, he has joy.

To clarify His point, Jesus proceeds to tell another short parable. The way this story unfolds is similar to the shepherd's tale. This time, it is not one hundred sheep and a shepherd but ten coins and a woman. But the point of the story seems identical. The actor in the parable is the woman. The lost coin (obviously!) takes no action. The climax of this story is about the woman's joy. It is about her joy in finding what she wants. When the woman finds what she wants, she has joy.

And let us be clear: although repentance is mentioned in both of these short parables, repentance is not what is being pictured. The lamb did not know it was lost; the lamb did not turn back to the shepherd; the lamb did not repent. And if that is not clear enough, think about that little lost coin. Clearly, we do not see, in these parables, any picture of how repentance happens—or even the need for repentance.

When you think about it, it makes sense. Jesus is not addressing the question of how one enters into the kingdom or how one should deal with offenses before God. What prompted these parables is the concern raised that Jesus hangs out with people the Pharisees and scribes would not hang out with. What is the answer to that concern? How does Jesus respond? He tells stories about having joy in finding what you want.

DID YOU HEAR THE ONE ABOUT . . .

Now we have the setting—the trajectory in the narrative—that gives rise to Jesus' longer parable. With these thoughts in mind, let us turn to the story about the prodigal. Keep in mind that Jesus is responding to a particular concern: why He hangs out with those He does.

And He said, "A man had two sons. The younger of them said to his father, 'Father, give me the share of the estate that falls to me.' So he divided his wealth between them. And not many days later, the younger son gathered everything together and went on a journey into a distant country, and there he squandered his estate with loose living. Now when he had spent everything, a severe famine occurred in that country, and he began to be impoverished. So he went and hired himself out to one of the citizens of that country, and he sent him into his fields to feed swine. And he would have gladly filled his stomach with the pods that the swine were eating, and no one was giving *anything* to him. But when he came to his senses, he said, 'How many of my father's hired men have more than enough bread, but I am dying here with hunger! 'I will get up and go to my father, and will say to him, *Father, I have sinned against heaven, and in your sight; I am no longer worthy to be called your son; make me as one of your hired men.'*

"So he got up and came to his father. But while he was still a long way off, his father saw him and felt compassion *for him*, and ran and embraced him and kissed him. And the son said to him, 'Father, I have sinned against heaven and in your sight; I am no longer worthy to be called your son.' But the father said to his slaves, 'Quickly bring out the best robe and put it on him, and put a ring on his hand and sandals on his feet; and bring the fattened calf, kill it, and let us eat and celebrate; for this son of mine was dead and has come to life again; he was lost and has been found.' And they began to celebrate.

"Now his older son was in the field, and when he came and approached the house, he heard music and dancing. And he summoned one of the servants and *began* inquiring what these things could be. And he said to him, 'Your brother has come, and your father has killed the fattened calf because he has received him back safe and sound.' But he became angry and was not willing to go in; and his father came out and *began* pleading with him. But he answered and said to his father, 'Look! For so many years I have been serving you and I have never neglected a command of yours; and *yet* you have never given me a young goat, so that I might celebrate with my friends; but when this son of yours came, who has devoured your wealth with prostitutes, you killed the fattened calf for him.' And he said to him, 'Son, you have always been with me, and all that is mine is yours. But we had to celebrate and rejoice, for this brother of yours was dead and *has begun* to live, and was lost and has been found'" (Luke 15:11-32).

You probably have heard this parable explained in terms of repentance. That what is being pictured—in the departure and return of the prodigal son—is a picture of what every person needs to do in order to come into life with God.

That common explanation suggests:

- Like the prodigal, we have offended our Father.
- Like the prodigal, we departed from Him.
- Like the prodigal, we try and satisfy ourselves with "worldly" resources.

- Like the prodigal, we need to come to our senses and realize what we have done.
- Like the prodigal, we need to return to the Father with an apology.
- Like the prodigal, the Father welcomes us when we return.
- Like the prodigal, we need to repent and confess and come back.

On the surface, this seems reasonable. But on closer look, the "model of repentance" approach to this parable seems incomplete—in fact, troubling.

Just notice and pay attention to how the story unfolds. The errant son "came to his senses" only in that he realized that he was needy and hungry and that his father had lots of resources that could meet his need. This young man crafted an apology—but it seems that it is only to try to get in good with his father. When he gets back to the father, this young man does not even get his apology out—the father interrupts him.

So if this is supposed to be a picture of repentance, it seems a very imperfect and incomplete picture. And remember what we have already seen. The words that lead us into the parable: "And He said . . ." What is implied? Why does the parable start this way? Jesus is *continuing* a thought, developing an explanation:

- "*So* He told them this parable . . . "
- "*Or* what woman . . . "
- "*And* He said, 'A man had two sons . . .'"

These three parables all address the same concern: the issue raised by the Pharisees and the scribes. They are, in a real sense, three verses of the same song. The first two verses are short; the third is longer. But they share many of the same features. Something is lost—one lamb out of a hundred, one coin out of ten, one son out of two. The primary actor in each is introduced right at the start—a man who is a shepherd, a woman keeping house, a father with two sons. Each of the stories ends with a celebration anchored in the joy of the primary actor.

Although the parable about the prodigal is a more detailed story, Jesus has not finished responding to the initial concern. Because of the way these stories are tied together in the context, because of the similar imagery in each, because each ends with rejoicing by the one who finds what he or she wanted, it would seem inappropriate to leverage the last parable of the three and make the point of that parable markedly different than the others.

So what can we conclude about how Jesus answers the charge that He is hanging out with the wrong kind of people? His answer is simple: Jesus hangs out with those He does for the joy of it! The shepherd finds what he wants and rejoices. The woman finds what he wants and rejoices. The father finds what he wants and rejoices. And Jesus is finding joy in keeping the company that He does. (And that includes us!)

BUT WHAT ABOUT . . .

So if we end up understanding the parable of the lost son this way, what are we to make of the older brother in the last parable of the three? If we keep in mind that parables often have details that help in making the point (but that are not the main point), we should be able to make sense of the older brother. He complains that the father has made much of the return of the "prodigal." But did you notice what the father's response was to his firstborn? "We [have] to celebrate and rejoice."

Some see, in the figure of the older brother, a not-so-veiled reference to the Pharisees and scribes who were critical of Jesus keeping company with those He did. But even if that is the case, I wonder whether it makes sense to hijack the trajectory of the three parables because of the reference to the older son. This interpretation is all the more unlikely, seeing that even in mentioning the older brother, Jesus' story still points to joy.

Now that we have given close attention to this parable (and the two that accompany it) we can hear Jesus' answer to His opponents. Each of the parables pictures the same thing: the joy of having what you want. And there we hear Jesus' answer: I hang out with those I do for the joy of it!

But you might be thinking, "I'm not a prodigal! I don't see myself fleeing from God. I do not squander what He provides. I'm not . . . "

That may be true. Perhaps the picture of the prodigal is not one with which you can identify. (You might not identify with the lost lamb or the missing coin either!) But that does not seem to be the point Jesus is making. Jesus is explaining why He chooses to be with the people He does. He is not so much describing the kind of people He hangs out with—or what they need to do to be with

Him—but is saying something about Himself. And whether you see yourself in the role of the prodigal or not, the answer Jesus offers could have a significant impact on the way you think of your relationship with Him. Jesus pursues you; He looks to have a relationship with you, He brings us into life with Himself for the joy of it.[58]

I remember speaking with a young Christian girl who was struggling, feeling stagnant in her life with Jesus. The more we talked, the clearer it became. She did, indeed, know the Lord. But she was not at all sure how Jesus felt about her. When I asked her how she thought Jesus felt about her, she paused, teared up a bit, and said, "I know that He loves me. That's what the Bible says." But when I pressed in a little further, it was clear that her sense of Jesus' love was more a cognitive assent to the biblical idea that "God loves me." There was little grasp of the richness, the passion, and the delight that flavors Jesus' love for her.

Like many followers of Jesus, she needed to hear clearly the message of the parable of the father who lost a son. It was not that she needed to know the need for repentance. She needed to know that the Lord loved her with a passionate, joyful, heartfelt, affectionate love![59]

REFLECTING ON THIS TRUTH

FOR PERSONAL REFLECTION:

1. With the way that this parable is often understood and taught, the emphasis falls on the need to be repentant and the steps needed to "get right with God."

There is, in Scripture, a proper place for repentance. But if we read this parable as substantially a call to repentance, what does that mean for the answer to the question of why Jesus shares life with those He does? If the crucial element of why Jesus pursues people is their appropriate repentance, how do we escape the conclusion that He loves us because we have done the "right thing" (thus, making His love for us something of a reward for our behavior)?

2. Why does it matter that we have a fuller and richer understanding of God's true affections toward those who are His? What would be the impact on your life if you lived with the idea that God's love is simply what He "must do" because, after all, "God is love"? How does it change the way you draw near to Him when you begin to grasp His joyful love for you?

3. It might seem strange to speak of God's "affections" when thinking about God's love. But the Scriptures are clear that God's love is not a cold, un-feeling decision He makes. In Zephaniah 3:17 (which might be good to read right now), the prophet gives voice to the Lord's love for His people. In that single verse, four different Hebrew words are used to refer to the exuberant joy that God feels for His people in His love for them. Take time to talk to the Lord about His affectionate, joyful love for you.[60] Ask Him to make it ever clearer; celebrate and enjoy His love!

FOR GROUP DISCUSSION:

1. How did you respond when the idea was raised that this parable is *not* about repentance? How hard is it to hold loosely that commonly embraced interpretation?

2. How does seeing the series of three parables tied together in the passage, help in understanding what Jesus is addressing? If you distilled the three parables down to one, single, compelling "punch line," what would it be?

3. Why would the religious leaders be so troubled by those Jesus was hanging out with? What does Jesus highlight as the reason for keeping such company? And most importantly, what does it mean for us to grasp the point that He made?

CHAPTER EIGHT

A BAD GOOD EXAMPLE

PRAISE FOR THE UNRIGHTEOUS MANAGER

"The sons of this age are more shrewd . . . than the sons of light."

Luke 16:8

I REMEMBER WHEN MY SON was just learning to walk. He was toddling around the house. Bracing himself by holding on to the furniture, he was getting pretty good at navigating the room. And then something surprising happened. He found my keys on the coffee table in the living room. I watched as he picked them up. I watched as he carried them away, pushing off from the table. And then I watched in surprise as he wobbled over to the front door, grabbed the doorknob, and started trying to get one of the keys into the lock.

I thought, *I didn't teach him about keys! How does he know what do with the keys?* Then it dawned on me. He had learned by watching—he learned from my modeling. He discovered, by simply observing, what keys were for.

Much of our learning in life comes that way. We learn from models—we learn through the examples of others. Fortunately, many of the models we learn from are good examples. We learn to tie our shoes, to make a peanut butter and jelly sandwich, to fold our hands when we pray, to communicate well, to serve others—all these things and more—from good examples.

But all the examples we will encounter are not necessarily good. We also learn from bad examples. That might sound a bit surprising, but a few moments of reflection will confirm that idea. We watch the driver heading down an icy road a little too fast skid out of control and tell ourselves that how he was driving is not a good way to drive. We notice the roommate in college who fails a class because she was up too late too many nights, goofed off in lectures, and was more interested in sorority activities than the homework. We learn something when a marriage is at risk because of the pattern of interaction between the spouses. We see a co-worker terminated for a poor work ethic and learn about what is *not* helpful.

All such examples—and many others—teach us by modeling how *not* to do life. They are good (that is, helpful) bad examples (of what *not* to do). So we learn from good examples. And we can learn from good bad examples. What is rarer is learning from *bad good examples.*

What is a bad good example? Put simply, it is a learning moment when we see someone doing something that, in itself, is not appropriate or right but that, in a certain context, provides us some insight into how to live well. It would not seem reasonable or right to take a pocketknife and a ballpoint pen and use them to cut into someone's throat. But there have been more than a few occasions when an off-duty doctor or an EMT did that very thing to save the life of someone who was in severe respiratory distress.[61] On one level, cutting into someone's neck in a fine restaurant would seem to be a bad thing. But when the situation is fully understood, this bad example turns out to be a good example of an unanticipated good intervention.

A LITERARY BAD GOOD EXAMPLE

Alexander Dumas wrote some great and notable novels. One of the most compelling is his story about Edmund Dantès, *The Count of Monte Cristo*. At the age of nineteen, Edmund appears to have everything going for him: a good job with a future in the merchant marine, a father who loves him, and a beautiful woman he will soon wed. But through a series of wicked and self-serving acts, a number of those who know him hatch a plot to have Edmund Dantès falsely accused of treason against the ruling party of France; and as a result, Dantès is exiled to life in prison.

Befriended by a priest imprisoned in the same penitentiary, Dantès becomes an educated man. When he escapes after the priest's death, he finds himself in possession of a great treasure deeded to him by the priest. With that education and the wealth that is now his, Dantès reintroduces himself into the world that he had been driven from. He comes to learn the truth about the conspiracy that overturned his life—and the names of those one-time acquaintances who spear-headed that conspiracy.

Unrecognized due to the passage of the years and the new persona he has adopted, Dantès sets his heart on a single thing—revenge.

On one level, the story is a very bad example of how to live. The priest had taught Dantès much—including the truth that justice and revenge must be left in the hands of God. But Dantès is so incensed at what others have done to him and how they had ruined his life, he cannot let go of the pursuit of vengeance.

Although it might be hard to determine what Alexander Dumas had in mind in penning this dramatic tale, there does seem to be a good example buried in this tale that seems to be almost entirely about a man who lives out a bad example. The good example is that it is possible to live for one thing.

Even though Dantès is doing a bad thing—living for revenge— that he can and does live for, one over-riding passion models something good—that it is possible for someone to be so captured by one thing that he lives all of life for that one thing. (And that, candidly, is a picture of what the Christian life should be like!) Thus, *The Count of Monte Cristo* gives us a bad good example.

The parable we will look at in this chapter is similar to that story—it is a bad good example. The principal character in the parable does something morally questionable (like Dantès), but Jesus uses the character's action to make a point about doing something good (like living for one thing seen in Dantès' story). It is not the badness that is being highlighted; Jesus is underscoring a way of thinking that, from His perspective, is actually good. So with that understanding of a bad good example, let us turn to the parable and read and listen well to find the good example Jesus is underscoring.

Jesus has been teaching and investing in those He had called to follow Him. He has a growing relationship with His disciples. Sometimes, He instructs them directly; sometimes, they learn by watching and participating. But they are growing in their understanding of what He wants for them as followers. After having spoken to a larger group of listeners about how the kingdom spreads,[62] Jesus has some words for His closer band of disciples.

> Now He was also saying to the disciples, "There was a rich man who had a manager, and this *manager* was reported to him as squandering his possessions. And he called him and said to him, 'What is this I hear about you? Give an accounting of your management, for you can no longer be manager.' The manager said to himself, 'What shall I do, since my master is taking the management away from me? I am not strong enough to dig; I am ashamed to beg. 'I know what I shall do, so that when I am removed from the management people will welcome me into their homes.' And he summoned each one of his master's debtors, and he *began* saying to the first, 'How much do you owe my master?' And he said, 'A hundred measures of oil.' And he said to him, 'Take your bill, and sit down quickly and write fifty.' Then he said to another, 'And how much do you owe?' And he said, 'A hundred measures of wheat.' He said to him, 'Take your bill, and write eighty.' And his master praised the unrighteous manager because he had acted shrewdly; for the sons of this age are more shrewd in relation to

their own kind than the sons of light. And I say to you, make friends for yourselves by means of the wealth of unrighteousness, so that when it fails, they will receive you into the eternal dwellings" (Luke 16:1-9).

On the surface of it, this is a troubling parable—some see it as one of Jesus' most puzzling[63]—because it sounds as if the parable lauds the morally unjustifiable actions of a manager of another man's business. After all, in the story, the master praises the man who cheated him!

In the introduction to our study of parables, attention was called to one of the essential characteristics of parables—they are like jokes. There is a punch line—even if the purpose of a parable is not to elicit laughter. And there is the "setup" for the punch line—even if the parable's setup seems somewhat true to life, it still is not functioning as a true story. In recognizing the way a parable functions like a joke, we must be careful not to get confused or caught up in the setup and thus miss the punch line. It is that interpretive framework that can help us grasp what Jesus was driving at in telling this parable.

Jesus was talking to His disciples. They have now been with him for some time. They have not only watched as He proclaimed the breaking in of His kingdom,[64] but they have also begun to participate with Him in the extension of that kingdom.[65] He has been leading them into what is involved in being a disciple.[66] And Jesus has been teaching them about the way the Father does and will care for those who are His followers.[67]

This parable is specifically addressing Jesus' disciples. He wanted them to grasp something more about what it means to be called into participatory "followership." This parable presents a bad good example of what Jesus wants for them. But without some careful reading, we might end up either being puzzled or even disturbed by the parable.

HE DID WHAT?

Look closely at the main character in this parable—the manager. What do you see? How do you think of him? Do you like him? Would you want this guy to work for you or to serve as the caretaker for your home? Let us just list some of the things that are clear about the man (remembering that this is not a report of what some person actually did but a description of a man for the purpose of making a point).

He had squandered the possessions of his employer. Squandering refers to an almost reckless scattering.[68] This apparently was not just an oversight or slip up on the manager's part—it is described as neglectful waste. He was self-serving and self-seeking. When he became aware that he had been found out, there is no evidence of a repentant attitude or a desire to make good on what he had lost for his master. There is no indication this manager wanted to work hard to turn things around with his master. He unscrupulously mismanaged his master's goods to ingratiate himself to his master's debtors. This goes beyond the squandering—this is using the goods of another for one's personal benefit.

If you were listening to this story for the first time, as Jesus told it, what would you think should happen to this wicked manager? How do you think the story *should* end? What is so surprising is that the master of the manager "praised the unrighteous manager because he had acted shrewdly." There is no getting around this. The master praises the manager. Shocking! The manager—who did so much wrong—is commended by his master—who had been cheated by the manager. That would have caught the attention of Jesus' disciples. And it should grab our attention as well.

Why the praise? What was the master calling attention to? (And what was Jesus calling attention to in telling this parable?) Clearly, the master was not praising the manager because he was immoral or wicked; he was not given a pat on the back for squandering his master's wealth or cheating the master out of what his debtors owed him. He was commended for *acting shrewdly.*

This word "shrewd" appears twice in this parable.[69] In other passages where the word appears in the New Testament, it is often rendered "wise." But it is not the only word translated "wise" in the New Testament.[70]

The manager is praised for being wise in a particular way. He understood the situation he was in; he saw what was coming; he realized that his actions in the present might have real impact on his future; so he acted accordingly. He was not being commended for being virtuous or noble—he was being congratulated for making the best of a bad situation (even though he did it in an immoral way).

This is the bad good example of the parable. Something bad was done; but in spite of the questionable moral nature of the action, Jesus affirmed that there is something good to be seen in this example. That is what must have caught the attention of Jesus' disciples—and it is what should capture our attention as well.

UNDERSCORING THE PUNCH LINE

We do not know how Jesus spoke these words. We do not know whether He gestured when He told this parable, where He raised His voice, or when He changed His pacing. In Luke's account of Jesus' words, he did not have the privilege of using italics or boldface type to place stress on certain words or phrases. But there are indicators in the text itself that aid us in noticing where the stress falls. And here, in this account, the little word *for* helps us.

"And his master praised the unrighteous manager because he had acted shrewdly; *for* the sons of this age are more shrewd in relation to their own kind than the sons of light" (16:8). In Jesus' story, the master praised the manager while still recognizing he was unrighteous; the master praised the manager not for what he did but for acting shrewdly. The "for" clarifies Jesus' perspective on what is essential. Shrewdness is commendable—and the "sons of this age" recognize the value of being shrewd. There is a kind of savvy attentiveness to how their world plays out that is seen in the way non-disciples carry out their lives. Seeing shrewdness as commendable, Jesus highlights the lack of this quality in the "sons of light"—His own followers.

If that is the punch line to this short parable, what are the implications? Fortunately, we are not left to guess because Jesus went on to offer some clarification for His disciples.

"He who is faithful in a very little thing is faithful also in much; and he who is unrighteous in a very little thing is unrighteous also in much. Therefore if you have not been faithful in *the use of* unrighteous wealth, who will entrust the true *riches* to you? And if you have not been faithful in *the use of* that which is another's, who will give you that which is your own? No servant can serve two masters; for either he will hate the one and love the other, or else he will be devoted to one and despise the other. You cannot serve God and wealth" (Luke 16:10-13).

Jesus turns from the bad good example pictured in the parable to straightforward instruction to those who long to follow Him. Initially, it might seem to be an abrupt change to go from picturing an unrighteous manager who acted shrewdly to talking about faithfulness, but there is a thread of continuity that ties the parable to these thoughts.

The shrewd manager used what was at his disposal for his greatest possible benefit. (Remember, he was not commended for being unrighteous but for making the most of his difficult situation.) Jesus' commentary focuses on using what is at one's disposal for one's greatest possible benefit. That would, in the language of the parable, be shrewd.

Jesus' call is quite clear: No one can serve "two masters." And, in particular, you cannot serve both "stuff"[71] and God. What does it mean to "serve wealth"? It is not that money or stuff or wealth issues edicts and commands, calling us to certain specific actions. But that does not mean people cannot be mastered by "stuff." Even if there are no commands issued or words spoken, the person who lives for stuff does live his or her life at the beck and call of that stuff. The priority given to having or getting or maintaining stuff is a kind of slavery to a master.

It is startling how we can minimize what Jesus said here. Jesus is not ambiguous. It is *impossible* to have two things equally sharing the place of primacy—the place of "master"—in life. Many seem to think Jesus was merely saying that having two masters is challenging, but that undermines what He said. It is impossible.

So how does that fit with the parable that preceded? A little thought brings it into focus. What is commendable about the manager in the parable was his shrewdness. That shrewdness was pictured in his making a decision about what was to be primary in his life—his own well-being or his master's well-being. Now it is *not* commendable that the manager was dishonest or immoral, but it *is* laudable that the manager decided to live for one thing. The manager in the parable was living out the reality that you cannot serve two masters.

The manager's shrewdness is seen in his clarity about this. Although the manager's opting to have his own self-interest be primary in his decision-making is not to be emulated, Jesus does say that the "sons of this age are more shrewd in relation to their own kind than the sons of light." This "son of the age" recognized the implications of living for one master—in his case, himself. The "sons of light" do not grasp the necessity of being attentively savvy in how life is lived—to do all they could to live for the one true Master.

It is easy to be a bit troubled by this parable because of the bad good example nature of the story. But once we have grasped the commendable thing captured by the parable, we might end up being even more troubled by what Jesus is underscoring. As a child of light–someone who has come into life through Jesus–will we live with such honesty and attentiveness to leverage all we have to live for just one master? How casual are we in thinking through the daily implications of what we are giving ourselves to? What fills our minds and hearts when we think about the day ahead is often a helpful indicator as to what we hold to be the master of our days. If Jesus and His kingdom are not often and readily at the top of list of what fills our minds and hearts, we are going to be torn between two masters. And that is an impossible way to live.

REFLECTING ON THIS TRUTH

FOR PERSONAL REFLECTION:

1. Jesus asks a compelling question with this sometimes-puzzling parable: are those who claim to follow Him living shrewdly? So pause and think. As you go through your days, are you honest and circumspect about how you are living? Do you ever take time to assess what you are doing with your time and resources?

2. What do you live for? What really functions as the "master" of your days? Have you defaulted to a kind of life that leaves you responding at the beck and call of lesser "masters"? Where does that happen? What could you do about quieting the call of those masters?

3. In one sense, there is a proper biblical call to live "selfishly." Jesus said that if you want to save your life,

you will have to give up your life for His sake (Matt. 16:25). Ask the Spirit to help you see what could change in the way that you are pursuing life so that you can more wholeheartedly, more shrewdly, more "selfishly," fully run after the life that Jesus has for you.

FOR GROUP DISCUSSION:

1. What do you find to be challenging or puzzling in this parable? Why do we struggle to make sense of this story Jesus told?

2. How does it help to remember that parables function like a joke? How do you distinguish between the punch line of this parable and the part of the parable that is simply necessary to set up that punch line?

3. How do you hear this parable with regard to your own life? Where does this parable prick or nudge you? In what way(s) have you fallen short of living shrewdly as a son or daughter of light?

CHAPTER NINE

GETTING (NOT) WHAT ONE DESERVES

LABORING FOR A SURPRISING LANDOWNER

"Is it not lawful for me to do what I wish with what is my own?"

Matthew 20:15

YOU HAVE PROBABLY BEEN ON the receiving end of lots of those kinds of calls.

"Hello! I have some great news for you. You have just received a free . . . "

As you listen, you know. The caller is hoping to draw you in. It might be for a visit to a timeshare. It could be that the hook being extended is an attempt to have you consider participating in a vacation club. You are eligible for a free home security system—as long as you pay for two years of monitoring service. You qualify for a free passive solar system—you only have to come up with the money to pay for the installation. And the free cruise—for all of three days—does not cost you anything, except half a day of your time and your endurance while sitting through a challenging "How can you pass this up?" offer to sign up for . . . You get the idea.

It happens often enough and is common enough that you would think telemarketers would realize it comes across as a little disingenuous. Most people already know that for all the promise of "free offers," there is always a price to pay. It is not that we are all cynical—hopefully, we are not—but the sales come-on has been used so often for so many things that we can readily become inoculated against the appeal. So we come to learn that "there is no such thing as a free lunch." We come to expect we should get what we deserve. We work for what we want, and we feel cheated if we do not get what we think our effort and investment merits. This thinking is common. Most of us have learned this lesson well.

But what if there really is an exception? What if there could be something truly free? It would be hard for us to see it. It would be a challenge not to slip back into incredulity, wondering what the catch was. It is right there—in the thought that there might be a different way to think about life—that Jesus' parables serve His hearers so very well. The parables Jesus told are often brilliant and insightful ways for His hearers to rethink how they have come to view how life works. He does not always make a frontal assault on the citadel of His hearers' preconceived and closely held beliefs. Sometimes, He slips behind the lines with a parable and overthrows the wrong thinking in a subtler—and more effective—way.

NOT A RANDOM "PEARL OF WISDOM"

As you reflect on Jesus' parables, it is important to notice that they do not hang out there on their own. Typically, a parable will fit in a flow of thought; parables are not isolated nuggets of insight like seashells you might find as you walk on the beach. It is also important to recognize that the chapter divisions commonly found in Bibles are not inspired.[72] Yes, that thought might seem shocking—as accustomed as we are to having the chapters and verses numbered. But recognizing the convenience of the versification while also recognizing that the chapter and verse breaks sometimes interfere with a good reading of the text is crucial. We should also admit that the chapter and section headings found in most Bibles are not inspired. The convenience of alerting readers as to what the next section touches on may seem helpful, but it can prove misleading.

Turning to the parable in view in this chapter, the only way to fully grasp what Jesus is saying is to notice that even though the parable appears at the start of a new chapter (and, typically, has its own section heading), Jesus is not offering a random pearl of wisdom. This parable comes at a particular place and for a specific purpose in the flow of what Matthew records for us.

So, what leads to this parable? A rather remarkable exchange occurs. It starts with a conversation between Jesus and a rich young man and follows with a conversation with His disciples, after which comes the parable. Let us step into that flow.

> And someone came to [Jesus] and said, "Teacher, what good thing shall I do that I may obtain eternal life?" And He said to him, "Why are you asking Me about what is

good? There is *only* One who is good; but if you wish to enter into life, keep the commandments." *Then* he said to Him, "Which ones?" And Jesus said, "YOU SHALL NOT COMMIT MURDER; YOU SHALL NOT COMMIT ADULTERY; YOU SHALL NOT STEAL; YOU SHALL NOT BEAR FALSE WITNESS; HONOR YOUR FATHER AND MOTHER; AND YOU SHALL LOVE YOUR NEIGHBOR AS YOURSELF." The young man said to Him, "All these things I have kept; what am I still lacking?" Jesus said to him, "If you wish to be complete, go *and* sell your possessions and give to *the* poor, and you will have treasure in heaven; and come, follow Me." But when the young man heard this statement, he went away grieving; for he was one who owned much property (Matt. 19:16-22).

At first read, this exchange might seem simple. A man asks Jesus what it will take for him to gain eternal life. Jesus tells the man that keeping the commandments is critical. After clarifying for the young man the commandments that are essential, Jesus tells the man that the only thing he still lacks is to let go of the material possessions he is clinging to and to follow Him. Simple and straightforward—only it is not.

LISTENING IN ON THE CONVERSATION

We will not be able to unpack everything there is to see in this exchange, but a couple of the main points will lead us toward insight into the parable that follows. We start with the young man's initial question: "Teacher, what good thing shall I do that I may obtain eternal life?"

What is implied in the question? The young man thought that there is something he could do to obtain eternal life—life with God. He thought that there must be some morally commendable tasks he could carry out that would procure that life.

Jesus' reply began with His own question. He asked why the young man wanted to know "what is good." He followed up that question by affirming that "there is only One who is good."[73] The point is that Jesus was prodding the young man to think well about what he meant by "good." Essentially, He was asking, "Are you really interested in knowing what is good from God's point of view?"

Given that starting point, Jesus continued. "'If you wish to enter into life, keep the commandments.'" Was Jesus telling this young man that he could earn his way into life with God by simply doing good things and by keeping the commandments? It initially sounds like that—even though, from other passages of Scripture, we come to know that no one can ever do enough good to merit life with God. But perhaps what Jesus was seeking to do becomes evident in how the man replied. "Which ones?"

This young man asked what he should do to obtain life. Jesus told him to (simply) keep "the commandments." So why did the young man ask the follow-up question he did? Apparently, he wanted to be selective about the commandments he would need to keep. And Jesus replied selectively.

In answering the man's question about which commandments to keep, Jesus turned to the well-known and highly regarded Ten Commandments.[74] But Jesus was selective. He only quoted the commandments that addressed relationship with other people;

He did not mention the commandments that addressed a person's relationship with God. Jesus was strategic in how He responded to the young man's question. He wanted the young man to think. But did that man think well?

The man's response gives us some indication. The man replied that he had, indeed, kept all of those commandments. But apparently, the man also realized there was something more. He asked, "What I am still lacking?" He seems to think something was missing in what he had, what he could control. He felt that lack.

Jesus' reply put the focus on the problem. There was not a lack—something to be supplemented. There was a surplus—something to let go of. "If you wish to be complete, go and sell your possessions and give to the poor, and you will have treasure in heaven; and come, follow Me.'"

Jesus' call does not appear to be a standard model for entering into eternal life. This man is the only individual Jesus called to sell everything and give it all away. And being attentive to Jesus' selective responses to the rich young ruler, it makes sense to see Jesus targeting something particular in what He said to this man. The call was to sell all his possessions. The word Jesus used speaks not just of property but would also include anything that would give the man an advantage—giving it all to the poor or presenting gifts to the temple or to others who could benefit the man after he had sold all. Jesus' call was for the man to dispossess himself of everything he thought gave him some advantage and indiscriminately give it all away to those who could not benefit him in any way. That was the right counsel to give to a man who had begun by thinking he could do something to merit, earn, or deserve eternal life: "No. You have nothing; you can do nothing that will indebt heaven to you."

As the rich young man walked away saddened by what Jesus had told him, Jesus turned to His followers and offered some commentary on the exchange.

> And Jesus said to His disciples, "Truly I say to you, it is hard for a rich man to enter the kingdom of heaven. Again I say to you, it is easier for a camel to go through the eye of a needle, than for a rich man to enter the kingdom of God." When the disciples heard *this*, they were very astonished and said, "Then who can be saved?" And looking at *them* Jesus said to them, "With people this is impossible, but with God all things are possible" (Matt. 19:23-26).

In a profoundly simple and compelling way, Jesus explained. Like many people in our day, the disciples thought that if someone had "stuff," he or she must be in favor with God—those with means were those who were friends of God. But Jesus contradicted that idea. Richness does not mean closeness to God or access to Heaven. In fact (offering a simple but often mis-explained mini-parable[75]), Jesus noted how impossible it was for a rich man to achieve kingdom life: it is as impossible as getting a camel through the eye of a sewing needle.

The disciples clearly got the point (no pun intended). They were astonished at the seeming impossibility of the image. And Jesus confirmed their astonishment. "'With people this is impossible.'" What is the "this" that is impossible for people? They cannot enter into the kingdom of heaven—procuring eternal life (like the rich young man was seeking). But Jesus affirmed that what is impossible for people is not impossible for God.

After a brief exchange with His disciples about what they left to follow Him (19:27-30), Jesus offered the parable we have in view. It comes in the flow of the story that has been unfolding. Jesus told the parable to provide some clarity to what he wanted the young man—and His disciples—to understand. The parable itself falls within a verbal parenthesis. Jesus' words that launch the parable are also the words that come at the end of the parable. That parenthesis points us to what we should attend to in the parable itself.

- "But many who are first will be last; and the last, first" (Matt. 19:30).
- "So the last shall be first, and the first last" (Matt. 20:16).

What do these words point to? Jesus is calling attention to rank, to value, to advantage—to the very things that had been shaping the rich young ruler's thoughts. And that idea is what leads us into the parable itself:

"For the kingdom of heaven is like a landowner who went out early in the morning to hire laborers for his vineyard. When he had agreed with the laborers for a denarius[76] for the day, he sent them into his vineyard. And he went out about the third hour[77] and saw others standing idle in the market place; and to those he said, 'You also go into the vineyard, and whatever is right I will give you.' And *so* they went. Again he went out about the sixth and the ninth hour[78], and did the same thing. And about the eleventh *hour*[79] he went out and found others standing *around*; and he said to them, 'Why have you been standing here idle all day long?' They said to him, 'Because no one hired us.' He said to them, 'You go into the vineyard too.'

"When evening came, the owner of the vineyard said to his foreman, 'Call the laborers and pay them their wages, beginning with the last *group* to the first.' When those *hired* about the eleventh hour came, each one received a denarius. When those *hired* first came, they thought that they would receive more; but each of them also received a denarius. When they received it, they grumbled at the landowner, saying, 'These last men have worked *only* one hour, and you have made them equal to us who have borne the burden and the scorching heat of the day.' But he answered and said to one of them, 'Friend, I am doing you no wrong; did you not agree with me for a denarius? Take what is yours and go, but I wish to give to this last man the same as to you. Is it not lawful for me to do what I wish with what is my own? Or is your eye envious because I am generous?' So the last shall be first, and the first last" (Matt. 20:1-16).

This is one of the Jesus' longer parables. There are lots of details. He offered a substantial amount of set-up leading to the punch line. Do not get lost in the details! As they heard this story as Jesus told it for the first time, how do you imagine those hearers were thinking as the story unfolded? Try and step into the moment, listening to the parable with fresh ears.

It begins with day laborers being hired for the day at the going rate. What would the hearers be thinking? Most likely something like, "That's reasonable. That's fair." But what would start to happen in their thinking as the story developed? Perhaps, "I wonder what those who began to work a few hours later will receive? How will the landowner fairly treat those latecomers?" And then we come to those who were brought on an hour before the workday ended. There must have been some internal calculations going on about what those workers would get.

When Jesus drew the story to a close and spoke of the owner giving a full day's wage to those who hardly worked at all, that ending was likely met with surprise. When those who worked the whole day got only a fair day's wage, the hearers would have responded like those in the story. There would have been some internal grumbling, a sense of "This is not right. That's not fair."

And with that, we come to the punch line. The turn in the story is what drives Jesus' point home: "Is it not lawful for me to do what I wish with what is my own? Or is your eye envious because I am generous?"

Although the hearers would have initially thought the story was about the workers because of the way the parable unfolds, Jesus made it clear that His focus is on the owner. The owner gets to do what he pleases with what is his. The owner can be as generous and gracious as he pleases, regardless of what someone might feel he or she is due. No matter how long someone labored—being "first" in line as a worker—or how late in the game one came—being "last" in line as a worker—Jesus says the kingdom works on a different economy. It is about the Owner's generosity and His willingness to do what He pleases with what is His own.

The rich young ruler, having all he had and having kept the commandments (at least some of them), felt he was due something. Or if it turned out that he still lacked something, he felt he could do what was needed to obtain his desired outcome—eternal life. But Jesus explained that the kingdom economy does not work that way. Those who feel they are at the head of the line, for whatever reason, are going to find that their advantages do not matter. And those who feel they are at the back of the line, for whatever reason, will hear good news: it is not about one's rank, or value, or advantage. Life in the kingdom is all about the Owner doing what He wants to do with what is His.

LOOKING BACKWARD TO SEE THE END

If we had been working through Matthew's entire Gospel instead of learning to read and understand parables, we would have picked up on an earlier moment that could help solidify what we have seen in this parable. Initially, it might appear to be a little disconnected piece of the story, but it actually launched the journey we have been on—taking us to the rich young man's encounter, into the impossibility of people obtaining kingdom life on their own, and on through to the parable.

An often-underappreciated encounter started it all: "Then *some* children were brought to [Jesus] so that He might lay His hands on them and pray; and the disciples rebuked them. But Jesus said, 'Let the children alone, and do not hinder them from coming to Me; for the kingdom of heaven belongs to such as these'" (Matt. 19:13-14).

These few verses prompt some questions:

- Why were children being brought to Jesus? What was anticipated?
- Why were the disciples opposed to the children being brought?
- In what way does the kingdom belong to those who are like children?

A little thought leads us to answers to these questions. Obviously, the children are being brought to Jesus because there is the anticipation that something good would come of it. The children would be prayed for, touched, and blessed by Jesus. They were there to receive something from Him.

The disciples were likely troubled because the blessing of children would have seemed to be a distraction from more important things. Even if Jesus blessed these children, they did not have anything to contribute to the ongoing ministry Jesus was engaged in.

Jesus' surprising proclamation brings this all into focus. The kingdom of Heaven—the experience of eternal life—belongs to "such as these" for the very reason that they come with no advantage, no claim, nothing to offer, no perceived value. They only receive from Jesus because the Owner can do whatever He wishes with what is His. He can be as generous as He wants; no one has a claim on Him. They are the "last ones" on nearly every possible scale, and for that reason, they are the "first ones" when it comes to the kingdom.

This is not a call to be childish; it is a declaration from Jesus that abandoning the idea of having some leverage is spiritually healthy. This is a call to childlikeness; it is a declaration from Jesus that those who come anticipating gracious benevolence from the Owner of the kingdom will not be disappointed. The rich young man did not come like a child. He came like a successful and competent negotiator, seeking to discover what leverage he might have to merit the blessings of life with God. Any person relying on his perceived advantages does not come as a child. That person will soon discover that all such efforts will prove as hopeless as forcing a camel through a needle's eye.

Jesus' kingdom economy only works on the basis of His generosity and His undeserved and unmerited kindness. Coming with no claim—coming as a "last one"—is really the only way to come.

REFLECTING ON THIS TRUTH

FOR PERSONAL REFLECTION:

1. You might not see yourself in the same category as the rich young man—you do not see yourself as wealthy. But as we have seen, it is not so much the riches but the attitude of the man that was in view. In what ways do you come to Jesus thinking that you have something—some virtue, some act of service, some obedience—that you subtly feel must give you a claim on Him?

2. If there were some human achievement or some personal resource that merited eternal life, where would the weight of experiencing kingdom life rest? Would that be good news? Why or why not? Why is it better news to know that entering into kingdom life is impossible for anyone by his or her own doing?

3. Where do you find yourself in this journey into life with Jesus? Are you just beginning? Have you been walking with Him for a few years, for a lifetime? What would it be like—wherever you find yourself— to embrace fully the implications of Jesus' parable: that all you enjoy—all the blessings—come entirely from His willingness to be generous to you?

FOR GROUP DISCUSSION:

1. What is the common theme reflected in the wealthy young man's concern and the way Jesus' disciples responded to His statement after the exchange with the young man? What were they all thinking? How widespread—in our time and culture—do you feel that thought is?

2. The wealthy young man went away sad. Why do you think he did not respond more positively to Jesus' advice? What was it in Jesus' call to the man that made it so difficult?

3. How does the parable Jesus told clarify what He was underscoring in His conversation with the young man? For the young man (and the disciples) the

parable touched on the subject of tangible wealth—but the call to "sell everything" is not the only possible implication of the parable. Where does that parable intersect your life?

CHAPTER TEN

WHAT IF IT REALLY WAS ABOUT THAT MOMENT?

THE VINEYARD OWNER AND THE TENANTS

"At the harvest *time, he sent a slave to the vine-growers."*

Luke 20:9-16

I REMEMBER A STORY I heard some years ago. It was about a mom of an elementary schoolboy. She came to pick him up when the school day was done and asked him how things had gone. After sharing a bit about the spelling words he learned and the games he played at recess, the little boy asked, "Mommy, where did I come from?" This question caught the young mom a bit off guard. She knew that one day, she would have this conversation with her son. But this was sooner than she had anticipated.

As they pulled into the driveway, she suggested they sit down for some milk and cookies at the kitchen table, and she would answer his question. Having settled in, she began. Delicately,

167

carefully, and a little cautiously, the mother walked her young and inquisitive son through a "birds and the bees" talk. She wished she had more time to prepare, but she did the best she could in the moment.

When she was done, she tenderly asked, "So, do you understand? I hope that wasn't too confusing. Do you have any questions?"

After a momentary pause, the boy replied. "Yes, Mommy, I think I understand. But I still have a question. At school, Jeffery said he came from Pennsylvania, and Margaret told me she came from Florida. Can you tell me where I came from?"

Humorous as it is, this little tale illustrates an important point—particularly when we are reading accounts of Jesus' interaction with people. We need to be clear on what question Jesus is answering. More often than not, Jesus' parables are part of a larger conversation. And very often, the parables are part of His response to a question that was raised. If we are not attentive to what the question was, we might misread the parable. We end up thinking that Jesus is talking about something other than what was in focus in the question.

When we read the Gospels, it is hard for us not to bring our already formed understanding to the text we are reading. We approach a passage thinking we know what is supposed to be happening; we feel reasonably sure we know what Jesus was doing and why. We can listen to His words with a kind of self-satisfaction that we see the point He was making—even before we have read attentively.

This is a common problem when we read about Jesus' miracles. There is a tendency to think that every miracle Jesus did was to prove that He was God. Now although it is true that Jesus is God come in the flesh, a careful reading of His miracles leads to the conclusion that maybe He was not "pulling out His God card" every time He did something miraculous.[80] When we think He was simply making that point, we can overlook what was really being revealed in and through His miracles.

When it comes to Jesus' parables, there is a similar common problem. There is a tendency either to think that every parable Jesus told was to clarify Who He is or that they are somewhat veiled sets of instructions for what we are to do. Having already looked at a number of parables, we have seen that is not the case. But we still have to resist hijacking parables to make them say those kinds of things. And the one we turn to now is one that is often read as if Jesus was intending to drive home His identity to His hearers. If we listen well to the question He was addressing and if we read attentively to how He replied to those who were there in that moment, we might come away with something a bit different.

ONE LINK IN THE CHAIN

Before we can turn to the parable that is the focus of this chapter, we will have to step back and take a look at what preceded Jesus' sharing what He did. That is the only way we will be able to grasp well the question that He was answering so that we will not misread the parable.

Luke tells us a great deal about what was going on in Palestine as Jesus approached Jerusalem. In Luke 19:29-38, we watch as Jesus approached the city, apparently at the time when many pilgrims were making the journey to Jerusalem. The crowd celebrated as

Jesus came riding into the city.[81] Although those who were gathered were not there solely to make much of Jesus, many were attentive to His presence in the crowd. Some spread their coats before Him as He came riding in as a sign of honor (19:36). And as He got nearer and people recognized Him and recalled the miracles which they had witnessed, they joyously praised God (19:37).

In Luke 19:39-44, we hear an exchange between Jesus and some of the Jewish religious leaders. They were concerned about what Jesus' followers were doing. They thought it inappropriate for them to praise God for Jesus when the focus of the feast was to be what God had done for the nation. Jesus not only affirmed the rightness of the celebration but also spoke of His sadness about the apparent inattentiveness of much of the city to what was happening in His arrival.[82]

In Luke 19:45-48, we catch a glimpse of Jesus as He drove merchants out of the temple and are told that He began to teach within the temple grounds. In turning the merchants out, Jesus referenced a couple of Old Testament texts as the justification for what He was doing.[83]

Over the course of the few days, a lot happened in the city. Jesus was at the center of quite a bit of religious fervor; His presence had created a stir. And He had, personally and intentionally, contributed to that stir. That is the setting for the exchange that leads us to a parable.

> On one of the days while He was teaching the people in the temple and preaching the gospel, the chief priests and the scribes with the elders confronted *Him*, and they spoke, saying to Him, "Tell us by what authority You are

doing these things, or who is the one who gave You this authority?" Jesus answered and said to them, "I will also ask you a question, and you tell Me: Was the baptism of John from heaven or from men?" They reasoned among themselves, saying, "If we say, 'From heaven,' He will say, 'Why did you not believe him?' But if we say, 'From men,' all the people will stone us to death, for they are convinced that John was a prophet." So they answered that they did not know where *it came* from. And Jesus said to them, "Nor will I tell you by what authority I do these things" (Luke 20:1-8).

We will need to grasp what is going on here if we are going to rightly understand the parable that Jesus tells immediately after this exchange. The question asked is clear; the religious leaders[84] wanted to know about Jesus' authority for doing what He was doing. Jesus had no official position in the temple; He was not part of the priesthood that ministered in the temple. Neither was He a member of the Jewish ruling council of the day. So in one sense, their question has some legitimacy.

In order to answer their question, Jesus posed His own question to them. He needed them to give Him a starting point for their understanding of authority. "'Was the baptism of John from heaven or from men?'" He was not asking a trick question; for Him to discuss authority with them, He needed them to provide some working definition. That could start with their assessment of John the Baptist and his very public and well-known ministry. If they would answer that question, Jesus could then build on that and respond to their question.

If you pay attention to what we are told about how these religious leaders reasoned, it becomes clear that they did not know how to settle on where authority comes from—from men or from God. Apparently, the only authority they could readily affirm was their own, hence the insistence that Jesus answer the question they had presented to Him. But without some sense of their grounding of authority, it would be nearly impossible for Jesus to answer their question satisfactorily. So He replied, "'Nor will I tell you by what authority I do these things.'"

Having anchored ourselves in the flow of the narrative, we can turn to the parable with a better chance that we will understand it correctly.

> And He began to tell the people this parable: "A man planted a vineyard and rented it out to vine-growers, and went on a journey for a long time. At the *harvest* time he sent a slave to the vine-growers, so that they would give him *some* of the produce of the vineyard; but the vine-growers beat him and sent him away empty-handed. And he proceeded to send another slave; and they beat him also and treated him shamefully and sent him away empty-handed. And he proceeded to send a third; and this one also they wounded and cast out. The owner of the vineyard said, 'What shall I do? I will send my beloved son; perhaps they will respect him.' But when the vine-growers saw him, they reasoned with one another, saying, 'This is the heir; let us kill him so that the inheritance will be ours.' So they threw him out of the vineyard and killed him. What,

then, will the owner of the vineyard do to them? He will come and destroy these vine-growers and will give the vineyard to others." When they heard it, they said, "May it never be!" (Luke 20:9-16).

One could find good Bible teachers who, in explaining this parable, read it primarily as an allegory: the owner of the vineyard is God; the tenants are the religious leaders; the servants are God's prophets; and the Owner's Son is Jesus.[85] Although I would not argue that such a view should be summarily rejected, I do not think that approach gives sufficient attention to the context in which Jesus told the parable.

Adopting such an allegorical approach, one could argue that the question of authority is answered by Jesus identifying Himself (in a roundabout way) as the Son of the Owner and that the religious leaders, in opposing Him, are rejecting the authority He has from God, the Owner.

Remember how we first explored the way parables convey their message. Like an arrow, there is a point and a shaft and feathers. The arrowhead is the key; the shaft and feathers help drive the point home, but we cannot let such things distract us from the business end of the parable. Similar to a joke, there is a setup and a punch line. We cannot get too deeply entangled in the setup; if we do, we risk missing the punch line.

Do not overlook where this parable ends. The story is not merely about tenants who reject the owner's authority. The climax comes with the affirmation that the owner will destroy the tenant farmers and give his vineyard to others. The point does not (simply) seem to be that the representatives of the owner have some delegated authority. The climax of the story is not (primarily) about identifying the last one sent as the owner's son. The point of the arrow appears to be that the owner can and will do with his vineyard whatever he wants. And if that is the proper climax of the parable, then perhaps the point of this story Jesus told is not about His identity.

Did you hear the response of the religious leaders when *they* first heard this parable? They say, "'May it never be!'" Why did they give such a reaction? You might conclude they thought it was terrible that the tenants in the story rejected and killed those sent by the owner. But if we keep on reading, we may discover a better reason for why they reacted with such shock.

> But Jesus looked[86] at them and said, "What then is this that is written: 'THE STONE WHICH THE BUILDERS REJECTED, THIS BECAME THE CHIEF CORNER *stone*'? Everyone who falls on that stone will be broken to pieces; but on whomever it falls, it will scatter him like dust." The scribes and the chief priests tried to lay hands on Him that very hour, and they feared the people; for they understood that He spoke this parable against them (Luke 20:17-19).

GAINING PERSPECTIVE

In responding to the religious leaders' troubled response—"'May it never be!'"—Jesus quoted from a psalm. The passage Jesus referenced comes from this section of Psalm 118 (it would be worth reading the whole psalm when you have a moment!):[87]

Open to me the gates of righteousness; I shall enter
through them, I shall give thanks to the Lord. This is
the gate of the Lord; the righteous will enter through
it. I shall give thanks to You, for You have answered me,
and You have become my salvation. The stone which the
builders rejected has become the chief corner *stone*. This
is the Lord's doing; it is marvelous in our eyes. This is
the day which the Lord has made; let us rejoice and be
glad in it. O Lord, do save, we beseech You; O Lord, we
beseech You, do send prosperity! Blessed is the one who
comes in the name of the Lord (Psalm 118:19-26).

This was a psalm that would have been familiar to these
leaders. It was one that would have been part of the body of songs
sung during feasts—the very feast that was being celebrated at
that time in Jerusalem as Jesus entered the city. In quoting a line
from the song, Jesus' hearers would have easily recalled the rest.
They would have remembered the heart of the message of this
psalm: the Lord (the God of Israel) is doing something. They
would have grasped Jesus' point—not that Jesus was (primarily)
making a case for His own identity but that Jesus was providing
the answer to the question they first asked Him and the question
He presented to them.

Jesus' ministry in Jerusalem was stirring troubling thoughts
in the minds of the religious leaders. The exchange Jesus had
with them raised the question of where authority comes from;
they broached the issue, and Jesus prodded them with His own
question. The parable then underscored the idea that there
is always a place where authority comes from: the owner. As

pictured in the parable, the owner rightly gets to do whatever he wants with what is his own.

That realization provoked the shocked response of the religious leaders; it dawned on them that God could do whatever He wanted with the temple, the Jewish system, and their activities.

Is that what God had been doing in and through John the Baptist? The religious leaders were unwilling to wrestle with that question. If the Lord God had been at work in John, might He also be working in and through this strange but compelling teacher Jesus? The religious leaders did not know how to face up to that. But they began to understand that if God was at work in and through those they would not have looked to, it was completely His right to do that!

BUT HE IS THE SON, ISN'T HE?

It is true that Jesus is the Son of God, sent into the earth to carry out the Father's will. So, on one level, when we insist that the message of this parable is about the tenants of the vineyard (the religious leaders) rejecting the messengers of the Owner (the prophets sent by God) and finally determining to kill the Son of the Owner (Jesus), this rings true—that basic idea is, in fact, biblically true. But we still need to wrestle with whether that was the primary point Jesus was making. Was His primary concern to address the issue of His own identity?

As we have seen, when we read this parable that way, we might not be doing justice to the context; we might be slipping out of the conversation where this parable is anchored. When we read this parable that way, we also distance ourselves from the impact it could have on our lives.

When we think the parable is about Jesus' identifying Himself, most Christian readers of the passage conclude, "I get it! They didn't see Jesus for Who He is. They are going to kill Him. How tragic. I'm so glad that I see it!" But if the heart of the issue is not identity but authority—that the owner gets to do whatever he wants with what is his—then the story might come home to us with fresh, and needed, impact.

Sure, we recognize Jesus for Who He is: the Son of God. Yes, we see the wickedness of those who killed the prophets and persecuted Jesus. But do we truly feel the weight of what Jesus is saying? If we do not read this parable well, we could easily distance ourselves from what might be the most important thing: God's ownership of our lives. What part of your life—of our lives—does God not fully own? He is not merely the Owner of the temple—the religious things you do—He is the supreme Owner of it all. And that means He gets to do whatever He wants with what is His.

I do not think that those of us who know Jesus as Savior and Friend and Lord need to worry about whether our salvation is at risk when we wrestle with the implications of this parable. But we might need to be honest with how we are living out the relationship with God that Jesus has brought us into. How do we feel when Jesus steps onto the scene of our lives and begins to change things up? What if He wants us to alter what we are doing—to not be in the relationships we are in, to change jobs, to go on a mission trip, to step up and serve others in some new way?

Sometimes, I can feel myself slipping into thinking, *By what authority are You messing with my life in that way, Jesus?* Do we live as if the sovereign God is the Owner of all that we are? Do we acknowledge that because we have been bought with a price, everything we do rightly falls under God's purview? Are we growing more and more comfortable with the idea that He can (and might) do with our lives whatever He sees fit? Consider the following passages that emphasize God's ownership of our lives:

- "Or do you not know that your body is a temple of the Holy Spirit who is in you, whom you have from God, and that you are not your own? For you have been bought with a price: therefore glorify God in your body" (I Cor. 6:19-20).
- "For not one of us lives for himself, and not one dies for himself; for if we live, we live for the Lord, or if we die, we die for the Lord; therefore whether we live or die, we are the Lord's" (Rom. 14:7-8).
- "Whatever you do, do your work heartily, as for the Lord rather than for men, knowing that from the Lord you will receive the reward of the inheritance. It is the Lord Christ whom you serve" (Col. 3:23-24).

REFLECTING ON THIS TRUTH

FOR PERSONAL REFLECTION:

1. Take time to make sure you understand what led up to this parable. Go back and read about what Jesus was

doing in Jerusalem. Pay attention to the tension between Him and the religious leaders. What really appears to be the crux of the matter? Would it have been enough for them to come to some conclusion about Jesus' identity, or is there something more to consider?

2. If we do not feel something of the shock the religious leaders did in hearing this parable, it might mean we have not grasped what Jesus was driving at. What keeps you insulated from feeling with them the impact of the parable? How might you distance yourself from the gripping nature of Jesus' story? Why does reading the parable as if it is about Jesus' identity rather than about God's authority insulate you from feeling the impact?

3. When you come to see the issue of God's authority and His right to do whatever He wants with what is His pictured in this exchange, how does the whole exchange come home to you? What does that realization do to the way you think about how you spend your time, steward your resources, and live in relationship with others?

FOR GROUP DISCUSSION:

1. What is the benefit of making sure we understand this parable (as with any parable) in the context in which it appears? How does what leads us into the parable and what follows help us not misread what Jesus is saying?

2. What best explains why the religious leaders were so shocked by the parable? If the point was primarily about Jesus' identity, do you think they would have responded as they did? Why or why not?

3. How does Jesus' reference from Psalm 118 help clarify the point being made by the parable He told? What is emphasized in the psalm? Why would Jesus have quoted that particular passage?

CHAPTER ELEVEN

THAT DID NOT TURN OUT SO NICELY!

THE UNWELCOME WEDDING GUEST

"But when the king came in to look over the dinner guests,
he saw a man there who was not dressed in wedding clothes."

Matthew 22:1-14

I THINK THAT IT HAPPENS with most children. In those early growing years, they carry around in their minds and hearts a particular picture of their parents. No one's cooking is as good as Mom's. She makes the best (fill in the blank)—cookies, sandwiches, soup, dinners. Dad can fix anything. He keeps the car running. The toaster does not burn toast anymore, and the water goes down the drain like it is supposed to. Mom always knows what to do when one of the kids is sick. Her attentive care heals little boo-boos, and her bedside manner can make the worst sick days manageable. Dad is strong enough to face any challenge. He is a great coach. He knows how to raise a puppy. And he kills spiders and other creepy crawling things.

But then, the children grow up. It is not that Mom and Dad have really changed all that much. But the little kids are no longer little, and their perspective of their parents grows with them. Mom's cooking is still good, but the best friend's mother's chili is "amazing!" And although Mom's homemade pies are as good as remembered, the bakery downtown offers delights that Mother never even would have tried. And an annual physical or a health checkup for sports makes it clear that Mom's tender care might need to be supplemented by some good medical assistance. Dad is still a good handyman, but he ends up hiring someone to fix things around the house he does not know how to tackle. And although Dad's cheering from the sidelines is still an encouragement, the team's coach has a better understanding of how to develop an athlete. Although the household insects are not too much for Dad, the squirrels in the attic make it clear that there are challenges that he cannot face without some professional help. So as children grow up, their view of their parents grows as well.

I think a similar thing happens as people grow in their relationship with Jesus. It is not that we come to see that He is not as good and competent and strong and resourceful and caring as we thought when we first met Him. Our perspective changes as we grow, but our view of Him does not diminish—it deepens and grows. But with that growth, there can also come some adjustments to our perspective. He is different than we first thought. Perhaps we first met Him as the One Who opened His arms to children who are climbing on His lap, and we view Him one way. And then we watch Him as He drives the moneychangers out of the temple in Jerusalem, and we have to add something to our view of Him. We first learn of Him as the One Who will rescue us out of Hell, and we view Him that way. But then we come to understand that it is not just the future that changes when we step into life with Him; He changes our present as well. And we grow in our relationship with Him as our view of Him matures.

The parable we will turn to next might be one of those perspective-changing, coming-to-see-Him-better moments. So let us read and listen carefully. But in order to get to that parable, we have to step into a moment of time with Jesus when tensions have been escalating between Him and the religious leaders.

WILLING TO ENGAGE

I once heard it said that Jesus was (and still is!) an "equal opportunity offender."[88] What is the idea? Simply put, that means in what He said and did, He often offended, in one way or another, both those who welcomed and embraced Him as well as those who struggled with Him and opposed Him. It was not that Jesus was obnoxious or trying to offend; but His understanding of life was so contrary to the way *everybody* saw things, there was a chance that both friends and enemies might take offense. Even when you see that happen and when people challenged or questioned Him, it is remarkable that Jesus continued to seek to engage them and help them think. He did not readily write people off. And He even did that with those who engaged in plots to kill Him!

As we approach this parable, Jesus had been teaching in the temple. His influence had spread greatly. Crowds gathered to hear

Him teach and came with their needs to receive a gracious touch from Him. His popularity was increasingly troubling to many of the religious leaders in Jerusalem. So when Jesus showed up in the temple and drove out those who had made the temple grounds a moneymaking bazaar, the leaders were even more offended. Those leaders challenged Jesus. They wanted to know why He thought He could do the things He was doing. He replied, seeking to engage them; but they pulled away. But Jesus did not leave it there. He told a parable, intending to stir them to think better about what they were doing. (We explored that parable and its implications in chapter ten.)

In reporting on this exchange, the Gospel writers let us know it did not go well. Matthew records, "When the chief priests and the Pharisees heard His parables, they understood that He was speaking about them. When they sought to seize Him, they feared the people, because they considered Him to be a prophet" (Matt. 21:45-46[89]).

What would you have done if your critics were stepping up their opposition? How would you respond if those who disagreed with what you were doing and saying were hoping to seize you to render you incapable of carrying out your plans? As mentioned, what is so wonderfully surprising is Jesus' continued intention to engage such opponents.

Matthew tells us, "Jesus spoke to them again" (Matt. 22:1). Although they wanted to finish off His ministry among the people, He was not finished engaging them. And the way He continued the conversation was by telling another parable.

> Jesus spoke to them again in parables, saying, "The kingdom of heaven may be compared to a king who gave

a wedding feast for his son. And he sent out his slaves to call those who had been invited to the wedding feast, and they were unwilling to come. Again he sent out other slaves saying, 'Tell those who have been invited, *Behold, I have prepared my dinner; my oxen and my fattened livestock are* all *butchered and everything is ready; come to the wedding feast.'* But they paid no attention and went their way, one to his own farm, another to his business, and the rest seized his slaves and mistreated them and killed them. But the king was enraged, and he sent his armies and destroyed those murderers and set their city on fire. Then he said to his slaves, 'The wedding is ready, but those who were invited were not worthy. Go therefore to the main highways, and as many as you find *there*, invite to the wedding feast.' Those slaves went out into the streets and gathered together all they found, both evil and good; and the wedding hall was filled with dinner guests. But when the king came in to look over the dinner guests, he saw a man there who was not dressed in wedding clothes, and he said to him, 'Friend, how did you come in here without wedding clothes?' And the man was speechless. Then the king said to the servants, 'Bind him hand and foot, and throw him into the outer darkness; in that place there will be weeping and gnashing of teeth.' For many are called, but few *are* chosen" (Matt. 22:1-14).

Perhaps the first thing we need to remember about reading parables is that they are not to be read as strict allegories. That is important for our making sense of this parable. Although we may be familiar with the ongoing revelation of God's plan presented to us in subsequent New Testament passages,[90] we should not conclude that either Jesus' disciples or the religious leaders would have understood this parable (with references to a king, a son, and a wedding feast) as an allegory about Jesus' own life and ministry. Jesus had not yet unpacked that idea for His hearers at this time.

That is not to insist there might not be some allegorical hints in this story, but we will miss the point if we think solely in terms of allegory. But if it is not an allegory, what then are we to make of this parable? Let us start by looking at the unfolding drama.

We do not have to allegorize the parable to see some significance for identifying the wedding party's host as a king. What does that mean for understanding this story? Well, simply put, the one extending the invitation is not just a friendly neighbor; the invitation extended was someone of great importance. This party is a big deal.

As was common in Jesus' day, an invitation was sent out (think, perhaps, of the contemporary practice of sending out a "save the date" notice before a wedding invitation is sent). Then came the day of the feast itself. The call went out; the time to celebrate had arrived. But those invited "were unwilling to come" (22:3). That is startling, worth noting. As the story opens, it isn't that the invited were unable to come (for some unspecified reason), but they chose not to respond, to not attend.

So the first call to come to the party was followed up with another. This time, the message made it clear that everything was ready. (Think: "Soup's on! Come get it while it's hot.") But the responses escalated. Some of those being invited paid no intention to the call;[91] others killed those extending the call.

The king was "enraged" at the response many made to the renewed call to come. His response to them was to kill those who had killed his servants and destroy the cities of those murderers. (Again, pay attention to the parabolic nature of this story. It would have taken some time to muster an army and mount up such attack. And by that time, dinner would have been cold!)

So another call went out but this time, not to those who were initially invited. Now the king's servants went out and gathered whomever they could—"both evil and good"—so that the wedding hall was filled.

Let us pause right there and try to get a grip on what is being underscored in this story up to this point. We cannot read this story as if it is an actual account of something that happened—the king pictured would have been a wicked and horrible king. And we should not spiritualize this story, moving toward an allegorical reading. With those things in mind, what does this parable picture (at this point)? A first-pass reading leads to this simple idea: invitations are not given idly. With the invitation, there is an expectation of participation.

As the parable unfolds, some do participate. But there is another surprising turn in the story. The wedding hall is filled—with a mixed group. In that group is a man who was not dressed appropriately for the wedding feast. Again, we get a clearly over-the-top response from the king. The improperly dressed guest in trussed up and thrown into a place where "there will be weeping and gnashing of teeth." (Why not simply ask the man to leave?) Jesus then wraps up the parable with a simple statement: "For many are called, but few are chosen."

ADDING IT ALL UP

Jesus' culminating statement should help us understand the point of the parable. But we will have to be careful to not read what we think we know from other texts into this passage. To refer to those who are "called" picks up on the opening sentences of the parable. The king sent out his servants to "call" those who had been invited. (In fact, the root word translated "called" appears five times in this passage; the other times, it is translated with the idea of invitation.)[92]

Part of what is most intriguing about this parable is that those who end up at the wedding feast include both the good and evil. When the king arrives, he does not remove any, except one man who was not dressed appropriately. He does not expel those who were "evil"—only the inappropriately dressed attendee. This suggests that perhaps this parable is not about ultimate spiritual salvation but about something else.

We already picked up on the thought that invitations are not given idly; the intention is that a call should elicit a response. But the parable also makes the point that there might well be an appropriate response and an inappropriate response (pictured by the person not dressed in a way that was fitting for the wedding feast). So remembering that Jesus is not only speaking to His followers but also to those who are not sure what to make of Him— to those who are somewhat antagonistic toward Him—what is

He underscoring? Could it be this question: "Are you responding appropriately to what you are hearing from Me?"

The broader context of His exchange with the religious leaders does not focus on extending to them a personal call to salvation, but it does include some provocative challenges to their thinking about how they were responding to Him. When we read this parable as if it is about "getting saved" or "getting into the eternal wedding feast," we might end up overlooking something a bit more fundamental. If we think, "I'm in; I accepted Jesus' invitation," we might lose sight of the importance of responding appropriately to everything He wants for us. If we think that having accepted Jesus' invitation to life means this parable does not have anything to say to us, we might be ignoring something significant. What if the parable is not about salvation (in the eternal sense) but about life—daily living in the presence of Jesus? What if it is not primarily speaking of eternal consequences but about feasting on what Jesus offers—or being left in sorrow and tears?

As Matthew recounts this parable for us, he moves directly from this exchange with the religious leaders to another exchange. Perhaps that subsequent interaction helps underscore the point of the parable.

> Then the Pharisees went and plotted together how they might trap Him in what He said. And they sent their disciples to Him, along with the Herodians, saying, "Teacher, we know that You are truthful and teach the way of God in truth, and defer to no one; for You are not partial to any. Tell us then, what do You think? Is

it lawful to give a poll-tax to Caesar, or not?" But Jesus perceived their malice, and said, "Why are you testing Me, you hypocrites? Show Me the coin *used* for the poll-tax." And they brought Him a denarius. And He said to them, "Whose likeness and inscription is this?" They said to Him, "Caesar's." Then He said to them, "Then render to Caesar the things that are Caesar's; and to God the things that are God's." And hearing *this*, they were amazed, and leaving Him, they went away (Matt. 22:15-22).

Jesus continues to engage with those who are resistant to Him and His ministry. They had sought to seize Him, but He spoke with them. Now they are trying to trap Him, and He continued to interact with them. But notice what is emphasized. They were trying to trap Him. The way they did this was to raise a question for Him they hoped He would not be able to answer without ending up in trouble. If He insisted it was not right to pay the tax to Caesar, it would end up raising concerns with Rome. If He insisted it was right to pay the tax to Rome, it would end up raising concerns among many of His followers, who, themselves, hated the Roman oppression.

He addressed those who raised the question. We are told Jesus perceived their "malice."[93] This does not mean they were as wicked as they could be; it does mean their motives were not good. He called them hypocrites. You likely have some image that comes to mind when you hear that word. But be careful to not read too much into it. The word occurs several times in Matthew and carries the idea of "acting"—doing something for "the show" or in order to make an impression.[94]

Why did Jesus call them that? They approached Him, affirming something they did not fully believe. They said that He was truthful; they said He taught the way of God in truth. But if they believed that, why would they seek to test Him? In this exchange, Jesus did not offer a parable. He told them the truth straight up: give to God what God should get. And that would seem to fit with the way we understood the parable. What God does and says—what Jesus said and did—requires a response. And there is an appropriate way to respond and an inappropriate way to respond. Respond to God as if He is God! Respond to what Jesus says and does as if that is what matters.

Clearly that would have implications for eternal life. But it provokes me more if I realize that Jesus was not speaking solely of responding to a "Gospel offer." Maybe Jesus was talking about everyday responses to the call of God through Him to live into life on His terms. For those who are not sure what to make of Jesus (like the Pharisees He was talking with), the parable is provocative: You have to do something with Jesus. You have to respond to what He does, what He says, Who He is. And there is a right way to respond and a wrong way to respond.

Some people, having heard of Jesus and having been, in some way, introduced to Him through a Christian friend or church, just set the whole question of what to do about Jesus to the side. Like the people in the parable, they are unwilling to respond to how Jesus might be inviting or drawing them. That might not even be an "invitation to accept Jesus as your Savior." It is simply that they cannot be bothered with Jesus. They do not want to consider Him and what He might be doing or might want from them. To not bother with Jesus does, in truth, have eternal consequences—serious eternal consequences. But the journey into a relationship with Him does not always start with the "big questions;" sometimes it just starts with being aware that He is there, in life, speaking and acting. And His very presence should provoke a response.

For those who do know Jesus, there can be a temptation to conclude this parable does not have anything substantial to say them. After all, they are "in;" they have accepted the invitation to the wedding feast. But if we are reading the parable well, it might not be about the saving invitation but about everyday kinds of moves of God in life. If we too easily conclude that Jesus is teaching about "getting saved" instead of living life, we could pass over the implications for our lives. It is simple—and provocative. Jesus regularly invites us. He invites us to greater dependence. He invites us into new aspects of serving. He invites us to a fresh experience of participation with Him in ministry. He invites us into deeper worship and more fervent prayer. He invites us into holiness and joy, into a life shared more fully with Himself.

And how do you respond? When you hear His voice, feel the nudge, know something is up, are you unwilling to respond to the invitation? That might not have the kinds of eternal consequences we associate with rejecting the call to surrender to the Savior, but an unwillingness to respond to the invitation to join the party hosted by Jesus might well leave us in a sad and unenviable place in life. To ignore Jesus' ongoing invitations to participate in life with Him might find us in a place of sorrow. Could it be that if you find yourself not fully enjoying your life with Jesus, you might have overlooked some specific invitation He has extended to you?

REFLECTING ON THIS TRUTH
FOR PERSONAL REFLECTION:

1. We can, at times, insulate ourselves from the things Jesus teaches and says. By importing what we think we know (even if those things are true), we can end up skipping over what Jesus says. Seeing as Jesus has not presented the idea of Him being the "Groom" nor any idea of a future "wedding feast," why should we be cautious in reading that idea into the parable we read in this chapter? How can that idea obscure what He might want to say to you?

2. If the point of this parable is more about responding to any and all of Jesus' invitations to participate with Him (rather than a call to salvation), what kind of impact might that have on your ongoing relationship with Him? Are any of His calls to you—any of His directions for how you should live with Him—secondary or unimportant? Are there any of His calls to you that you have been negligent to attend to?

3. When Jesus finishes up His interaction with His opponents by speaking about making sure one gives to God what God deserves, where does that idea intersect with how you are living daily life? Would you say that

God is receiving from you all that is appropriate? Can you say that you are not withholding anything from Jesus in your life with Him?

FOR GROUP DISCUSSION:

1. When reading this parable, why is it critical to keep in mind whom Jesus was speaking to and what they would, or would not, have known about Him and His ministry? Why is it important to *not* read our thoughts about Jesus as the Divine Groom and the Church as His bride into this passage?

2. We can easily dismiss Jesus' opponents; we conclude we are nothing like them. But could there be times when we really are a little dismissive about what Jesus wants for us? Is there a way that this parable could possibly speak to those times we are a bit neglective in our response to Him? Where might you feel that in your life?

3. The follow-up comments that Jesus made to those who brought their question about taxes can help confirm how we are not understanding the parable. Although we might not see ourselves as antagonistic toward Jesus as we perceive those religious leaders who questioned Jesus, how critical is it that we also "give to God what is God's"? How do we, at times, resist living into that?

CHAPTER TWELVE

IT MAY MATTER MORE THAN IT SEEMS

THE RICH MAN AND LAZARUS

"If they do not listen to Moses and the Prophets,
they will not be persuaded even if someone rises from the dead."

Luke 16:31

SOME PEOPLE THOROUGHLY ENJOY THEM; others cannot stand them. Most people have tried, at least a time or two, to put a jigsaw puzzle together. Some such puzzles are incredibly challenging, with thousands of pieces; others are simple, with a clear picture and only a few dozen pieces. Typically, those who enjoy a jigsaw challenge have a strategy for tackling the assembling of the parts. Some begin with the edge pieces, laying out the boundaries and the corners and filling in other pieces from the edges while working toward the center. Other puzzle-solvers pick out a particularly prominent part of the puzzle and start by finding the pieces that fit that part, matching colors and shapes.

Whichever approach is taken, there are a few common "rules to the game," so to speak. The pieces all need to fit together; forcing individual pieces in is a great way to ruin the puzzle. Even if you have a piece that seems to fit a particular shape, if the colors and images do not line up, it might be a good piece but it is in the wrong place. Without some attention to the overall picture of the puzzle, just butting pieces up next to others where they seem to fit will not complete the puzzle.

When reading a passage of Scripture, we are not trying to assemble a jigsaw puzzle. It is not as if the biblical authors have presented us with a challenging conundrum that will require some elaborate strategy to read the text with understanding. But when we are reading a portion of Scripture, those basic "rules of the game" for working a jigsaw puzzle can provide some appropriate guidelines for reading well.

Forcing an idea on a passage or attempting to make a text fit some preconceived notion of what the particular text *must* have meant is a sure way to ruin one's understanding of the passage. And if, when reading and making sense of a specific section, the idea in mind does not line up with the context in which the passage is found, you might be thinking of a broadly biblical idea. Still, it might not be what the particular passage has in view. It is possible—and happens all too often—for good biblical ideas to be "taught" from texts that do not speak to that particular truth.

This can easily occur when we read or listen to a parable of Jesus. Because these stories have been widely shared (and widely mis-remembered) apart from the context in which they appear, we can end up turning the particular piece that is the parable over and over, trying to make it fit somewhere in our understanding of Jesus' teaching. But the best way forward will be to fit the parable into the space it occupies in the flow of the Gospel in which it is found. We do not need to force it to fit, nor should we ignore the pattern and shape of the context in which it is found. Holding to those "rules of the game," we can rightly understand what Jesus was saying and the implication of the parable for our own lives.

Let us listen to the story.

> "Now there was a rich man, and he habitually dressed in purple and fine linen, joyously living in splendor every day. And a poor man named Lazarus was laid at his gate, covered with sores, and longing to be fed with the *crumbs* which were falling from the rich man's table; besides, even the dogs were coming and licking his sores. Now the poor man died and was carried away by the angels to Abraham's bosom; and the rich man also died and was buried. In Hades he lifted up his eyes, being in torment, and saw Abraham far away and Lazarus in his bosom. And he cried out and said, 'Father Abraham, have mercy on me, and send Lazarus so that he may dip the tip of his finger in water and cool off my tongue, for I am in agony in this flame.' But Abraham said, 'Child, remember that during your life you received your good things, and likewise Lazarus bad things; but now he is being comforted here, and you are in agony. And besides all this, between us and you there is a great chasm fixed, so that those who wish to come over from here to you will not be able, and *that* none may cross over from there

to us.' And he said, 'Then I beg you, father, that you send him to my father's house—for I have five brothers—in order that he may warn them, so that they will not also come to this place of torment.' But Abraham said, 'They have Moses and the Prophets; let them hear them.' But he said, 'No, father Abraham, but if someone goes to them from the dead, they will repent!' But he said to him, 'If they do not listen to Moses and the Prophets, they will not be persuaded even if someone rises from the dead'" (Luke 16:19-31).

IS IT A PARABLE OR NOT?

As we turn our attention to Luke 16:19-31, we have to answer a basic question: Is this story of Lazarus and the rich man a parable? Within the scholarly community, there is some debate; some insist this is a parable akin to other parables of Jesus, while others argue that this is more historical and realistic.

Some Bible teachers observe that the text does not tell us this is a parable[95] (as often happens in accounts of Jesus' teaching[96]). Although some take this to be a decisive observation in driving the conclusion this story is *not* a parable, there are several stories of Jesus that *are* regarded as parables that do not include any mention that we are about to hear or read a parable. The Gospel writer, and not Jesus Himself, often indicates that the account we are reading is a parable. A parable does not need a headline telling us what it is.

Another argument for this particular story not being read as a parable is to notice that we are given the name of one of the people in the story; it is argued that Jesus never does this in any of His parables[97] (as you may have noticed in the other chapters in this book). The idea is that for Jesus to identify a particular man, He must be referring to an actual historical event. But do not overlook that Jesus did not name the rich man; he is simply identified as "a rich man." It could also be that the name "Lazarus" was not a reference to a particular poor man but that the name was signifying something; the name "Lazarus" means "God is helper."[98]

Some suggest that what characterizes Jesus' parables is that they present something like a hypothetical situation, not a true-to-life picture.[99] It is argued that this story does not fit that style of teaching. However, although the story does begin with what could be read as a true-to-life picture, there are several features in the story that, when read attentively, cannot be picturing something that actually happened.

In support of reading this story as a parable, we only will need to note the features of the story that do not correspond to life as it is. Are we to assume (as is mentioned in the story) that the departed dead still have physical bodies (before the final resurrection), that those in a place of torment can see and converse with those who are in a place of rest and blessing, and that Abraham is a mediator of post-death conversations? Those who argue for reading this story as a historical account have to shift their thinking about these aspects of the story as symbolic. But if those critical pieces of the story are to be read and understood symbolically, why should we not read the whole story symbolically (or parabolically)?

With some clarification about the nature of this story, we can make better sense of the parable. We will have to get an initial understanding of what Jesus is saying to His hearers in this parable before we attempt to fit it into where it belongs in the larger passage. As with all parables, we want to look for the main idea and not get too caught up in the details of the story.

In the account, we meet three individuals: the rich man, Lazarus, and Abraham. What are we told about each? The rich man lived in joy, lived well-clothed, lived luxuriously. He is not pictured as wicked or irreligious; we are only told he lived a well-provisioned life. Although we might assume that the rich man should have known about the poor man "at his gate," there is nothing in the story that suggests he had intentionally ignored him.[100] Lazarus, in contrast, is described as one who lived destitute, as a beggar, in suffering. He is not pictured as either righteous or religious; we are only told he lived a hard existence. All we know of Abraham, in the parable, is that the rich man recognized him and believed that Abraham could provide him some help. It is worth noting that Abraham, who is not in the same after-life place as the unnamed rich man, was himself identified as a rich man in the Old Testament.[101]

We are told that both Lazarus and the rich man died. Notice the metaphorical way Lazarus' death is described. Angels carried him away bodily while we are simply told the rich man was buried. Both are then pictured in a place of life after death. Hades, the destination of the rich man, was a word used by the Jews to refer to the place of the departed dead; it is not necessarily to be equated with the Christian view of Hell.[102] To speak of Lazarus in "Abraham's bosom" is a way of saying that he was where Abraham was; it is not necessarily to be equated with the Christian view of

Heaven.[103] It is in that scene, in the time after death, we are told of the rich man's request for help.

Initially, he asked for mercy—to have his thirst quenched through Lazarus coming to where he was to give him a taste of water on his lips. That request was refused; Abraham explained it was impossible for anyone to travel from one part of the afterworld to another. But this is followed by another request: that Lazarus be sent to his brothers so they could avoid the afterlife torment the rich man was enduring. This request was also refused—in a surprising way. Abraham declared that even if someone were to return from the dead, people would be unpersuaded (apparently, about conditions after death) if they were not already persuaded by what Moses and the Prophets had written (a reference to the Old Testament Scriptures).[104]

So, what does this puzzle piece show us? What part of the overall picture is Jesus offering? Is He telling His hearers something about Heaven and Hell? Is the parable about how to earn or deserve Heaven by carrying for those less fortunate, or are less fortunate rewarded in exchange for the suffering they have endured in life?

As with other of Jesus' parables, the "punch line" comes at the end.[105] This parable closes with an affirmation of the necessity of listening to what the Old Testament Scriptures reveal. Although the life situation of the rich man and Lazarus and how their final destination is portrayed differs, the parable's point would seem to be that whatever the Scriptures affirm must be understood and embraced. The culminating idea is not about doing good with your stuff or enduring while suffering to get to a better place after death but about paying attention to the Scriptures while one has the opportunity.

LOOKING FOR EDGE PIECES

This parable is part of a larger narrative. It fits into an ongoing conversation that Jesus was having with His disciples and some religious leaders (who spoke up during that conversation). Attentiveness to how the parable began helps underscore this context: "Now there was a rich man" (16:19).[106] That word "now" is not to be understood in a temporal sense ("now in this moment of time") but in a logical sense ("now let me explain this to your further"). We will, therefore, be helped in understanding the point and place of this parable by taking a closer look at the context in which it is found. And to do that, we will have to back up a bit and get a running start.

As Luke 15 opens, Jesus addresses the concerns raised by some of the religious leaders. In that chapter, we have the report of Jesus' parables about the man who lost and subsequently found his lamb, the woman who lost and subsequently found her coin, and a man who lost and subsequently found his son. (See chapter seven for a discussion of these three parables.) The essential message of those parables is that Jesus does what He does, seeking those who are His, for the joy He has in finding them. Those parables help us understand Jesus' own mission—why He did what He did.

Chapter sixteen opens with Jesus turning His attention to His disciples: "Now He was also saying to the disciples" (16:1). This is where Jesus taught His disciples the need to be shrewd—to live purposefully and attentively for that which matters most—as we noticed in the parable of the "unrighteous [or shrewd] manager." (See chapter eight for a discussion of that parable.) After stressing to His disciples that they need to be shrewd in all they do as His followers, Jesus told them to use what they have of the world's goods to make headway for the sake of the kingdom and the life to come.

We then get a profound and compelling call from Jesus.

> "He who is faithful in a very little thing is faithful also in much; and he who is unrighteous in a very little thing is unrighteous also in much. Therefore if you have not been faithful in the *use of* unrighteous wealth, who will entrust the true *riches* to you? And if you have not been faithful in *the use of* that which is another's, who will give you that which is your own? No servant can serve two masters; for either he will hate the one and love the other, or else he will be devoted to one and despise the other. You cannot serve God and wealth" (Luke 16:10-13).

Stated simply, Jesus is underscoring what we could call the "two masters problem." It is not just challenging to attempt to multitask life's priorities by giving oneself to two different ultimate centers of life. Jesus says to try to live as if there are two primary or essential masters is an impossibility. No one is capable of living that way. Having clarified for His followers the one thing He Himself is living for, having called His followers to be shrewd themselves in how they think about kingdom life, and then having underscored the impossibility of seeking to live for both God's kingdom and human wealth, He is then interrupted by some religious leaders. Apparently, they had been listening in on that conversation with the disciples.

REALLY? YOU MUST BE JOKING!

Although the religious leaders of the day were not fond of Jesus' ministry and teaching, they did hang around Him, listening in as He taught and watching what He did. The next moment in Luke's narrative points this out.

> Now the Pharisees, who were lovers of money, were listening to all these things and were scoffing at Him. And He said to them, "You are those who justify yourselves in the sight of men, but God knows your hearts; for that which is highly esteemed among men is detestable in the sight of God. The Law and the Prophets *were proclaimed* until John; since that time the gospel of the kingdom of God has been preached, and everyone is forcing his way into it. But it is easier for heaven and earth to pass away than for one stroke of a letter of the Law to fail. Everyone who divorces his wife and marries another commits adultery, and he who marries one who is divorced from a husband commits adultery" (Luke 16:14-18).

Having made His point that it was impossible to serve wealth and serve God, the religious leaders scoffed. Apparently, they were convinced they *could* serve two masters. Luke tells us that they were lovers of money; that would mean—from what Jesus had just said—they could not be lovers of God. Jesus charged them with seeking to be seen right in the eyes of men—that is the sense of "justify yourselves in the sight of men." They wanted to look like appropriately pious leaders in the eyes of other people. However, He clarified that God knew what was going on in their hearts. These religious leaders were living for what was highly esteemed and valued by men while ignoring the things that were of the greatest importance in God's kingdom. Jesus stated that what they were pursuing was detestable in God's sight.

It might seem that Jesus then abruptly changed subjects as if He had lost the thread of His discussion with them when He mentioned John and the message of the kingdom. But perhaps that is not the case. When Jesus referenced the Law and the Prophets,[107] He was speaking to them about what they would have known, the Scriptures they knew. At first read, it might appear Jesus was setting up the Old Testament Scriptures in opposition to His own message of the kingdom. But closer attention to what He said clarifies that was not the case.

The Law and Prophets pointed to something, and that something was the kingdom that Jesus was now proclaiming. John the Baptist appeared on the scene, announced the breaking in of God's kingdom in a fresh way and pointed others to Jesus as the Mediator of that present kingdom. In one sense, we could say the "pointing" of the Old Testament was over. (This is why, in Mark 1:14-15, we hear Jesus declaring: "The time is fulfilled, the kingdom of God is at hand.") Jesus then clarified that with the proclamation of the present kingdom, people were diligently pursuing it, seeking to enter in.[108]

But even with the breaking in of God's kingdom in a fresh way through Jesus' ministry, this did not mean that the Law and

Prophets were either faulty or worth neglecting. Jesus affirmed that nothing in the Law was "fail-able." But the Law and the Prophets had a purpose; they pointed to God's plan—a plan that was coming to fruition in a profound and new way in the person of Jesus.

So why did Jesus then raise the issue of divorce and remarriage? It does not appear that anyone had raised that concern with Him at this time. Keep in mind that Jesus is still addressing the Pharisees' interruption; He does not turn His attention back to the disciples until the first verse of chapter seventeen.

In other passages, we can find Jesus addressing the issue of divorce.[109] Some of the religious leaders challenge Him to resolve what they thought was a thorny problem regarding divorce and remarriage. So, the issue of divorcing one's wife was a not uncommon matter of debate for the Pharisees. And the Pharisees typically pitted their personal take on the issue over the plain teaching of the Old Testament. They sided with those who wanted to end their marriage over what God had clearly said. That is a symptom of the "two masters problem." We might pick up on what Jesus was doing in making that reference if we listen carefully.

Having walked through the exchange, we can more easily outline the flow of thought.

1.   Jesus called His followers to be shrewd (16:1-9).
2.   That shrewdness looks like being faithful and living for just one master (16:10-13).
3.   The Pharisees, seeking to live to please both men and God, scoffed at Jesus' call (16:14).

4. Jesus pointed out that the Law and the Prophets pointed to the one kingdom that had come (16:15-17), supporting the call to live for God alone.

5. As an example of how the Pharisees sought to please both men and God, Jesus gave the example of their handling of divorce (16:18).

6. And at that point, Jesus told the parable with which we are wrestling.

Reading attentively, one picks up patterns of thought and phrases that help us fit the puzzle piece of the parable into the greater picture. In talking about being shrewd, Jesus explained that living shrewdly with earthly goods would result in being welcomed "into the eternal dwellings." That appears to be pictured in the parable of the rich man and Lazarus. In explaining the parable of the shrewd servant, Jesus spoke of not living for wealth but for God alone—the "two masters problem." He called attention to the very thing the Pharisees struggled with.

In pointing out the need to live for the one thing that mattered most, Jesus underscored the idea that the Law and the Prophets pointed to that one kingdom. And in the parable, Abraham asserts that the writings of Moses (the Law) and the Prophets were sufficient to point anyone toward the truth of what to live for—if they were willing to "hear them."

All this leads to the conclusion that the parable of the rich man and Lazarus is not a call to merit salvation by using one's wealth to care for the poor but a call to heed what the Law and the Prophets pointed to so that, hearing their message, the "two masters problem" could be resolved. But if that problem is not resolved in a person's life, the consequences would have an eternal impact.

AN INTERRUPTION

We have looked at what led up to Jesus' telling this parable, but it is also beneficial to notice what immediately followed: "He said to His disciples, 'It is inevitable that stumbling blocks come, but woe to him through whom they come! It would be better for him if a millstone were hung around his neck and he were thrown into the sea, than that he would cause one of these little ones to stumble'" (Luke 17:1-2).

Jesus is picking up the conversation He had been having with His disciples when the religious leaders interrupted. In one sense, Luke 16:14-31 is a side discussion stirred by the scoffing of these leaders when Jesus raised the "two masters" issue. The narrative flow would be relatively unaffected if we followed along with Jesus as He was speaking to His disciples about His own priorities, the need for His followers to be shrewd in living for His kingdom, the importance of recognizing the "two masters" problem, and then picking up on Jesus' warning about stumbling blocks that they would have to face.

In the midst of that flow, we have the exchange with the religious leaders that closes out with the parable in view. What is central to that side discussion is the necessity of listening to and heeding the message of the Law and the Prophets that point to the breaking in of the kingdom through the life and ministry of Jesus. To reject Jesus, to scoff at Him, is anchored in a disregard to what the Scriptures clearly declare. If one is not willing to listen to the Scriptures and pursue the kingdom of God as it is stated there, even a resurrection will not be convincing.

One of the underappreciated moments in the parable is when the rich man cries out to Abraham for mercy (16:24). What is startling about this cry is that the man does not call out to God for mercy but to "father Abraham."[110] (This is particularly notable if we remember that the name Lazarus means "God helps!") Who is the man looking to for what he needs? Has the rich man resolved the "two masters" problem for himself?

Although we have noted that the picture of the afterlife presented in this parable does not necessarily correspond to what life after death is like, what the rich man says is an important part of the puzzle. He turns his attention to what Abraham might be able to do for him. Jesus noted that the Pharisees were those who "justify [themselves] in the sight of men," appealing to what was "highly esteemed among men" (16:15). Apparently, they were overlooking the highest and most important call found in the Old Testament:

- "You shall love the LORD your God with all your heart and with all your soul and with all your might" (Deut. 6:5).

- "Now, Israel, what does the LORD your God require from you, but to fear the LORD your God, to walk in His ways and love Him, and to serve the LORD your God with all your heart and with all your soul" (Deut. 10:12).

- "Moreover the LORD your God will circumcise your heart and the heart of your descendants, to love the LORD your God with all your heart and with all your soul, so that you may live" (Deut. 30:6).

But this interruption—and the parable Jesus told—could also speak to us if we listen carefully. There will be times in our journey with Jesus when we hear something from Jesus presented in the pages of Scripture that we find hard to embrace or a bit too challenging or seemingly unreasonable. At such moments, we might scoff. We might be a bit dismissive of what Jesus tells us.

He cannot really mean it is impossible to "serve two masters." We do that (or think that we are doing that) much of the time. He cannot mean we will have to choose between being wholly devoted to God or being given over to some other ruling passion in life. He cannot be suggesting that our choices to make life more pleasant on our terms (like the way the Pharisees treated divorce) is that much an affront to God. Jesus cannot mean that if the way we are living life is tainted by our desire to be perceived as accepted and affirmed by those around us we might be at risk of living in a way that God despises. Does Jesus truly intend to suggest that if we settle for the kind of life approved by others, we might miss the kind of life God wants for us? That failing to resolve the "two masters" problem is to trip over a stumbling block that prevents us from seeing what the Scriptures point to and what Jesus calls us to?

But what if Jesus really *does* mean to say all those things? What are the implications of this exchange with the religious leaders? Could it be that the parable of the rich man and Lazarus is not really about "getting saved," but about seeing what matters most?[111] Could it be that the parable is not calling us to evaluate whether we are wealthy like the rich man or destitute like Lazarus but about paying attention to what the Scriptures (the Law and the Prophets) tell us about the kingdom that is now present and that being willing to live, every day, for one master is what is most important?

Jesus' parable is neither a condemnation of riches out of hand nor an unqualified promise of blessings for the destitute. He is highlighting the importance of God's Word—Moses and the Prophets—in resolving the "two masters" problem. He is underscoring the need for all who hear to attend to the Scriptures and believe what they call for. R. C. Trench rightly noted, "The rebuke of unbelief is the central thought and aim of this parable."[112]

REFLECTING ON THIS TRUTH

FOR PERSONAL REFLECTION:

1. It is common—and all too easy—to overlook what Jesus is saying to a particular group of people in the Gospels when we do not think of ourselves as identifying with those with whom He is speaking. In this passage, we can easily pass over the implications of what He said to the Pharisees, telling ourselves we are neither religiously prideful nor overly concerned with wealth. But we do not have to completely identify with the Pharisees to hear something from Jesus in this text. What caught your attention? What do you think Jesus wants you to grasp or see in the telling of this parable?

2. How have you come to grips with the "two masters" problem in your own life? Are you willing to embrace Jesus' radical statement that to live for two masters is

actually impossible? In what ways do you attempt to tame what He said so that the parable—picturing the seriousness of the consequences of not resolving that issue—will not trouble or stir you too much?

3. Where and when have you scoffed at something Jesus said? In what ways are you dismissive of what He might be telling you? Are you willing to let the Scripture (for the Pharisees, that would be the Old Testament; for us, all of the Bible) point you to what is essential for life? What stands in the way of your more fully embracing what God, through His Word, is calling you to?

FOR GROUP DISCUSSION:

1. Hopefully, putting the pieces of this passage together has not been as challenging as a jigsaw puzzle. Why is it important to see the "interruption" that occurs in the conversation that Jesus was having with His disciples? How does that shape the way we should hear and understand the parable?

2. The Pharisees were listening in on Jesus' conversation with His disciples. Hearing what they did, they scoffed (and interrupted) Him. The flow of the narrative would lead us to believe that Jesus picked up His discussion with the disciples after that interruption. How would they have made sense of and applied what they overheard Him say to the Pharisees? When Jesus turned His attention back to them, He warned them

about "stumbling blocks." In this context, what might a stumbling block be?

3. When Jesus first turned His attention to the Pharisees and at the end of the parable, Jesus called their attention to the Scriptures—the Law (or Moses) and the Prophets. Why that emphasis? What is He underscoring for them? What should we take away from what He is stressing?

EPILOGUE

HOW THE PARABLES OF JESUS CAN HELP US

"And all were speaking well of Him, and wondering at the gracious words which were falling from His lips."

Luke 4:22

MY SON, CHRISTOPHER, IS A professional stage actor. Over the years, my wife and I have seen him in many productions. He is particularly impressive when he does Shakespeare—he does it so well. But truth be told, when we see him in a Shakespeare production, it is initially a bit challenging. Although he is speaking English, he is not speaking in the way we commonly think of English being spoken. That is not surprising because he is using the Bard's words! But we must be particularly attentive to ensure that we are not missing something or overlooking something or mishearing what is being said.

It could be said that when listening to a classic production, contemporary theater-goers might think, "Never has a man spoken the way this man speaks." That is, most people do not

215

speak like Shakespeare wrote. (That is, by the way, what makes his plays so wonderful and compelling.) I am not suggesting that Shakespeare's words rise even minimally close to the words of Jesus, but the idea that the playwright did not write the way *I* might have said something is important to recognize.

When we turn to the Gospels and begin reading and listening to Jesus, we might too easily slip into thinking that He should say things the way we would. We think Jesus ought to have expressed Himself, told stories, used illustrations, and clarified what He was teaching in ways that fit the way we think. But something happens when we begin looking closely at His teaching—and, in particular, His parables.

Jesus does not say things the way we might; He does not speak the way others around us do. And although He often explains what He means, He might not do it in the way it is commonly done in the world around us. As Jesus taught, those who listened were often "amazed at His teaching" (Matt. 7:28, 22:33; Mark 1:22). It is not that they had not heard good teaching before, but there was something markedly different about how He spoke and what He said. This is why when the religious leaders sent guards to arrest Jesus, they could not! "'Never has a man spoken the way this man speaks'" (John 7:46).

So, how can a study of Jesus' parables help us? If we recognize that there is something different and compelling about Jesus' words and teaching, we might look to pay greater attention to what He said. If in our study of His parables we see that our habit of slipping into thinking we know these stories actually leaves us missing out, we might start considering that maybe, just maybe,

Jesus *will not say things the way we would.* If we begin to think that way about the words and teaching and parables of Jesus, we could find what He said to be compelling and life-changing. And as we listen well and read well and think well about what we find in Jesus' teaching, we might find fresh faith growing. This is exactly what happened to Jesus' listeners in the New Testament: "As He spoke these things, many came to believe in Him" (John 8:30). So here are a few suggestions to keep listening to Jesus well:

READ THE GOSPELS

It is not that other books (like this one!) or Bible teachers and pastors are not beneficial. But do not lose sight of the power of Jesus' words—and give yourself to hearing exactly what He said simply and clearly. Even the best teachers sometimes misconstrue Jesus' words, so be a diligent reader for yourself.[113] Even this book is not intended to be an end in itself; it was written to press you, the reader, into the Gospels and help you engage with Jesus' words for yourself. Nothing should take the place of your own personal reading, contemplating, and wrestling with Scripture.

THINK WELL

Whenever you read something that Jesus said or did, do not start with the assumption that you already know what He was communicating or what He was doing. Yes, you might have heard some (or even much) of the Gospel accounts before. But if you do not give yourself to slowing down and thinking well about what you find on the pages of the Scriptures, you are likely to miss something life-changing. Thinking well and deeply about what you find in your reading is an important part of spiritual growth.[114]

CALL ON THE SPIRIT

Jesus spoke. The writers of the Gospels put pen to parchment and recorded what He said. But they did not do that on their own.[115] The Spirit of God guided and preserved the record of Jesus' teaching. But that is not all the Spirit did or does. He also can help us better understand what we read and hear from Jesus.[116] Do not hesitate to ask the Spirit, Who inspired the Gospels, to aid you in understanding the Gospels. This does not mean we can bypass reading well with the expectation that the Spirit will download truth to us apart from the words on the page. But the transforming power of Jesus' words is experienced by those who read His words under the direction of and with the help of the Spirit.

TALK WITH OTHERS

Not one of us always reads and understands Jesus' words perfectly. We all have biases and blind spots. The way we have heard a parable or something Jesus taught explained might keep us from being appropriately attentive. Inviting others into your exploration of Jesus' words can help you see what you overlooked, pick up on something that escaped you, and nudge you to consider something you would rather avoid. Sharing with others what you are seeing and hearing from Jesus is a great way to grow in understanding what He says.[117] So open the Gospels. Read Jesus' words. Listen carefully. Invite the Spirit's help. Talk over with others what you see and what you are learning. And become ever more impressed with Jesus!

APPENDIX A

USING THIS BOOK IN A SMALL GROUP SETTING

"They were continually devoting themselves to the apostles' teaching and to fellowship, to the breaking of bread and to prayer."

Acts 2:42

MANY CHRISTIAN COMMUNITIES HAVE COME to realize the benefit of small groups. These are settings where Christians can gather to discuss and reflect on the Scriptures together, where individuals are free to ask questions and share thoughts, and where believers can pray into their own lives the truths they learn. Small groups are a helpful piece of the discipleship puzzle.

With years of experience with small groups, I am convinced that every gathering of saints will benefit greatly from living together in the Word. Like the early church that was devoted to "the apostles' teaching," healthy small group life grows out of a life shaped by the message of Jesus and the truth of Scripture. Such thinking has shaped the writing of this book.

Two of the primary goals in preparing this material are to help others think well about what Jesus taught, particularly in the parables He shared, and to encourage others to pay attention to what they read in the pages of Scripture and to become better readers of the Gospels.

With those goals in mind, it may be that this collection of reflections could be of benefit to a small group in their study and discussion of Scripture. But in order to keep the main thing the main thing, the following suggestions are offered for using this book in small groups:

1. Do not lose sight of the primacy of the Scriptures. Each chapter in this book does contain portions of the Bible under discussion. What matters most are the words the Spirit inspired—the words of Scripture. The words of this author are neither inspired nor life-changing—God's Word is. So however this book is used, it should be as an auxiliary to the Scripture, not in place of the Scriptures.

2. Do not overlook the value of reading Scripture together. Reading, listening to, and talking about the Scriptures is of vital importance. Even if the participants in the group have read the particular text in view, when it comes time to meet, reading the passages from the Bible and discussing what is there in the pages of the Bible should take priority. What insights might be found in this book should only be welcomed to the degree that they arise clearly from the Scriptures.

3. The group discussion questions at the end of each chapter are neither mandatory nor inspired. They are suggestions. They are intended to prompt interaction about what Jesus Himself taught and what the parables themselves were intended to convey. If the questions are helpful, feel free to use them. If they are not, you are obviously free to come up with your own.

4. Do not hesitate to debate, discuss, or disagree with what you read in this book. What matters most is that we grow to understand the Scriptures well and grow to know Jesus better. Allow the chapters in this book to nudge you toward those ends—even if you do not see eye to eye with this author. If in the end, we disagree but you have wrestled well with what Jesus said as recorded in the Gospels and you have come to be more impressed and more in delighted in Him, then this book will have served its purpose well.

PARABLES AND OTHER LITERARY FORMS

His disciples said, "Lo, now You are speaking plainly and are not using a figure of speech."

John 16:29

ONE OF THE CRITICAL ISSUES in defining and understanding parables is to recognize the boundary that separates a parable from other literary forms. A parable differs from an *allegory* in that although they both are illustrative stories seeking to make a point, a parable will use words with their natural sense in telling the story while an allegory uses the words and details in the story in a metaphorical way. In other words, unlike in a parable, the people, places, and events that make up an allegory stand in for other things outside the story world. Paul Bunyan's *Pilgrim's Progress* is an example of an extended allegory.

A parable differs from a *fable* in that although they are both intended to make a particular point, a parable will use true-to-life situations and people in telling the story, while a fable uses fantasy characters and highly imaginative situations to make the storyteller's point. In other words, unlike in a parable, the people, places, and events found in fable are not realistic. The stories of Aesop are examples of fables.

A parable differs from a *myth* in that although they both are illustrative stories, a parable uses real-life characters and situations to awaken real-life implications, while a myth builds the story with elements that—although they may parallel things in the real world—are part of a foreign or imagined world. In other words, unlike in a parable, the world of the myth is populated by unrealistic beings. The stories associated with classic Greek mythology are examples of this kind of literature.

Some stories have blurred boundaries, sharing features of more than one kind of literature. C. S. Lewis' *The Chronicles of Narnia* seem to share features of both allegory (recognizing the author's intention for people and events in the story to stand in for things in the real world) and myth (seeing that lessons being taught are often learned in an imaginary world).

A parable, being a figure of speech based on a comparison or contrast, is similar to both a *simile* and a *metaphor*. Although there is some overlap in how these figures of speech are understood, they are not identical. It could be said that a simile is a kind of metaphor, but it is not true that all metaphors are, in fact, similes.

Commonly, a simile contains the word "like" or "as" (or their equivalent) and, in making a comparison, identifies some attribute(s) of one thing as an attribute(s) of another. For example, in the film *Forrest Gump*, Forrest is heard repeating something his mother had said: "Life is like a box of chocolates, you never know what you're going to get."[118] The idea of variety and surprise that is associated with a box of chocolates is pictured as how life plays out. In a metaphor, similarity is depicted but without any necessary transfer of attributes. For example, to write, "My heart is breaking over the loss of my love," there is no transfer of attributes; neither is the writer's physical heart in view, nor is there any actual breaking occurring. The idea of loss and damage to one's emotions is a picturesque image for the strong feelings being endured.

For discussion of the basic meaning of the word "parable," see Robert H. Stein's *An Introduction to the Parables of Jesus* (Philadelphia: Westminster Press, 1981), 15-21. For additional study on the subject of literary forms in Scripture, see Howard G. Hendricks and William D. Hendricks, "What Type of Literature is This?" in *Living by the Book* (Chicago: Moody Press, 19910, 209-19).

APPENDIX C

THINKING ABOUT THE "BIG STORY"

He was speaking the word to them, so far as they were able to hear it.

Mark 4:33

IT IS COMMON TO HEAR—FROM many sources and many teachers—about the need to grasp "the big story of the Bible." The idea is that one needs not only to know what the big story is but also that apart from knowing the big story, one cannot read and understand Scripture.

Sometimes, the approach is presented by way of an analogy of a jigsaw puzzle. The Bible is a collection of little stories—the pieces of the puzzle. To make sense of what one is reading (an individual piece) one has to have the box top in view. Without the box top—without the big story already in place—the argument is that it will be hard (if not impossible) to understand the pieces.

If it is necessary to have the big story of the Bible in mind in order to understand what any particular passage in the Bible is about, where do we turn to get that big story picture? Where is the box top we need in order to know how to assemble the puzzle pieces? Those who advocate a big-story approach to reading the Bible do not seem to be able to point to any specific passage where their idea of the big story can be found.

If it is necessary to begin with the big story of the Bible in mind to understand God's revelation, why did He choose to reveal His truth "in many portions and in many ways" (Heb. 1:1)? Why did God reveal His plan in such a way that all the pieces were not given at one time (Eph. 3:5)? Those who advocate a big-story approach to reading the Bible do not have a way of explaining how those who were living in the story of the Bible could have made sense of what God was doing in and through them. They also lose sight of the need to understand each passage, as it stands in Scripture, on its own terms.

If we privilege the big story of the Bible approach to Bible reading where every passage is read through the lens of what we already believe to be the message of the Scriptures, how will our view of what God is doing in the world ever be corrected by Scripture? The religious leaders in Jesus' day seemed to think they knew what God was up to in the world (a version of the big-story approach), and yet they could not make sense of Jesus and His ministry. Jesus encouraged them to read Scripture (Matt. 21:16; Mark 2:25; and others). He did not start by explaining to them His understanding of the big story of the Bible.

It might just be that God's intention—in providing us His revealed Word in the way that He has—is that we simply start reading, somewhere, and grow to understand the Scriptures step by step.

REFLECTIONS ON READING THE GOSPELS

AVOIDING THE SCHOLAR'S STUMBLE

*"Thus invalidating the word of God by your tradition which you
have handed down."*

Mark 7:13

THIS APPENDIX IS NOT AS much encouragement in how to
read the Gospels well but a call to be aware of what one might
encounter in Bible study materials found either in print or online.
If you do not anticipate you will ever pull out a commentary or
listen to a university Bible teacher explain a Gospel passage, you
might not need to read this appendix.

In my studies in the Gospels over the years and in various
academic settings, I have heard things that sound like the following:

- The words attributed to Jesus in the Gospels were
  probably not all spoken by Him.

- The Gospel writers pulled together things they heard that Jesus said and did and imaginatively wove them together into their respective narratives.
- Some of Jesus' words found in the Gospels are quite possibly creative works of the Gospel writers themselves, expressing what they wanted their readers to know about how they thought about Jesus.

How should a committed student of Jesus' words and works understand such assertions, particularly when voiced by those with academic credentials, faculty positions at Christian universities, and published books to their name? Certainly, there are things that we can learn from those who write and teach in schools of higher education. But after years in that academic milieu, I am aware of both challenges and stumbling blocks. Whether it is listening to a professor or reading a highly recommended commentary, awareness of some of the tendencies in the academic study of the Gospels can guard you against becoming mired in troubling thoughts and assertions.

UNDERSTANDING THE ACADEMIC CULTURE

Pursuing doctoral studies in the Gospels, I was somewhat surprised by the assumptions that were common and the perspectives that were championed. Listening to conversations, engaging in classroom discussions, and working on a dissertation, there were clearly acceptable ways of discussing the Gospels and other ways that were often looked at askance. I found that it was not common to speak or write about what Jesus said or did. One had to refer to what a particular Gospel reported Jesus said or did. And even that needed to be carefully worded. One could not speak of what Mark or Matthew wrote, but the way to speak was to refer to what the author of the Gospel attributed to Mark or identified by the name Matthew wrote.

There was a whole way of thinking and referring to what we find contained in the Gospels that was shaped by a long-standing and widely held academic perspective. It was as if a series of lenses were inserted between the words we have in the Gospel records and the reader. And those lenses were often unconsciously embraced while simultaneously altering how any Gospel text was read.

To understand this culture, we have to take a look back at the history of the field of New Testament criticism as it has shaped academia. The science of New Testament criticism is relatively new. "Critical" study of the New Testament books (e.g., questions of authorship, date, canonicity, etc.) was not entirely absent among early students of the Bible. Even some of the early church fathers addressed some of these issues. However, New Testament criticism really came into its own in the nineteenth and twentieth centuries.

In the early nineteenth century, rationalism, the dominant philosophy of the day, began taking a hold in New Testament scholarly circles. The New Testament writings began to be read with an anti-supernatural bias. Man's reason became the arbitrator of authenticity and authority with regard to what is found in the New Testament. With a growing skepticism of even the possibility of the miraculous happening in life, new ways of making sense of the Gospels came to the forefront.

It was during this time that academicians in seminaries and religious schools influenced by this rationalism turned their attention to the "Synoptic Problem." (The word "synoptic" comes from the idea of "seeing together" and arises from the observation that the first three Gospels cover much of the same material; they "see together" Jesus' life and ministry.) At its center, the Synoptic Problem is the attempt to describe the relationship between the first three Gospels. The perceived challenge was how to explain the similarities and differences between these three Gospels recognizing that the accounts they share of the miracles of Jesus could not be records of what actually happened—given the perspective that the supernatural does not happen.[119]

SOURCE CRITICISM

The effort to address this problem focused on various theories about literary dependence between the Gospels. This could explain how the Synoptic Gospels could record similar accounts of things (like miracles) that the critic knew could not have happened. Various hypotheses were advanced, arguing for various sources for what ultimately found its way into the Gospels. Oral stories about Jesus, scattered and piecemeal written records, and familiar collections of memorable sayings were all considered the fertile ground which the "evangelists" (who were assumed not to be eyewitnesses to the events written about—because no one could be an eyewitness to miracles that could not happen) drew on in writing what they did. This endeavor gave rise to what is known as Source Criticism.

There is not universally accepted solution to the Synoptic Problem, although at times, one view tends to carry more weight than the competing alternatives. The "Two Source Theory" is widely accepted (even by some more conservative scholars). Put simply, this hypothesis suggests that the author of the Gospel of Mark, drawing on what was available to him, wrote the first "gospel" that told some things about this enigmatic figure named Jesus. According to this theory, the authors of Matthew and Luke then drew on what they knew of the Gospel of Mark and, with additions from a document called "Q" (from *Quelle*, the German word for "source"), wrote the Gospels that bear those names. It is worth noting that although this is a commonly held view, there is no manuscript evidence for any such "Q" document.

FORM CRITICISM

Source Criticism focused attention on the use of certain written documents that were assumed to be behind the canonical Gospels. However, it did not clearly address the origin of such sources. Questions ultimately arose regarding what preceded these written sources. Form Criticism, drawing on some form of Source Criticism theory, sought to explain how the oral tradition was preserved, circulated, and finally formalized. The Form critic's task was to analyze the "forms" found in the written Gospels in an attempt to ascertain what units of oral tradition might lie behind the written accounts and, subsequently, to classify and assess those forms. Although there may be some limited value in reflecting on such issues, in the hands of the more persistent

Form critics, this approach became a process for evaluating the historical validity of the identified units of oral tradition. The presuppositions that were introduced in this process gave way to the trends often found in New Testament studies today.

Form Criticism begins with a not-altogether-erroneous assumption that there would likely have been various oral reports of Jesus' words and deeds circulating freely after His death. But building on that idea, the argument was made that as these stories were retold, they were modified and embellished (and even in some cases created wholesale) by the Christian community to meet specific immediate needs. Well-known Form critics like Martin Dibelius[120] and Rudolph Bultmann[121] [122] embraced a view of that oral history process that led them to categorize many such "forms" as myth or legend—creations of the believing community—thereby denying the historical validity of those accounts.

TWO KINDS OF TRUTH

For Bultmann and others who have followed in his footsteps, there are two types of history. *Historie* is made up of that which is external, objective, and verifiable—real space-time events. *Historie* is objective history. *Geschichte* consists of events that are perceived to be true in the mind or heart; this history is internal and non-verifiable and constitutes the "faith" or subjective history of the believing community. There is no need, to this way of thinking, for *Geschichte* truth to be rooted in *Historie* truth. Like mythic tales that present moral truths, the *Geschichte* truth found in the Gospels needs not have any objective connection to *Historie* events. This results in a New Testament scholar asserting that something encountered in the Gospels is "true" in the sense that it gives rise to a beneficial and life-affirming way of thinking about life that need not be "true" with regard to the facts of objective history.

Thus, for the Form critic, underneath the Gospel records, there might be a Jesus of history (*Historie*). However, after His death, the reports of His life and teaching (and "supposed" resurrection) circulated, were modified and altered, and finally accepted and put into written form, creating the Christ of faith (*Geschichte*). The task for the Form critic became to "demythologize" the Gospels, to work from the Jesus of faith pictured in the Gospels and to resurrect from those accounts something that could be affirmed as genuinely true about the historical figure Jesus.

REDACTION CRITICISM

Similar to the way Form Criticism was an outgrowth of Source Criticism due to Source Criticism having left some questions unanswered, Redaction Criticism began to play a role in the 1950s out of apparent shortcomings of Form Criticism. The Form critic, with his emphasis on the creative community giving shape (or "form") to the oral traditions, could offer no adequate explanation for the individual characteristics of each of the Synoptic Gospels. With Form Criticism, the evangelists were simple collators of the forms found in the sources.

The Redaction critic suggests that the distinctives found in each Gospel are attributable to the evangelists. According to Redaction Criticism, the authors of the Gospels were not simply collectors of the material they found in their sources—they were authors/editors ("redactors") in their own right. The argument is made that they took the various units (in "forms") available to them and arranged, modified, altered, and even created new material in order to prepare something for the community in which they lived. All this was done with particular theological purposes in mind— purposes in the mind of the evangelist and not necessarily in the mind of Jesus (if the evangelists could even know what had been in the mind of Jesus). This results in the evangelists being seen as primarily theological creative writers and not as historians. It is assumed that the immediate needs of their respective communities and their own personal theological biases would render it virtually impossible for them to serve as good historians.

WHERE DOES THIS LEAVE US?

Thus, beginning with an anti-supernatural, rationalistic foundation, the Source critic attempts to identify the sources for the Synoptic Gospels. The Form critic then explains how those sources grew out of the creative oral traditions concerning Jesus. The Redaction critic then proposes how the evangelists constructed their respective Gospels, altering and creating along the way in order to fit their personal theological perspectives. Ultimately, this leaves the scholar in the driver's seat. Based on how he understands the resolution of the Synoptic Problem and drawing on the results of New Testament Criticism, the scholar assesses both the authenticity and accuracy of what is read in the Gospels and presents his case for how and why a particular passage found its way into a particular Gospel.[123]

Such a view is at odds with what the Christian community has held for most of its history. From the earliest days, there are writings that confirm the eyewitness nature of the Gospel accounts.[124] The church has affirmed that the Bible tells us truthfully and accurately what Jesus said and did. Although not an exhaustive record of His life (John 20:30), the Jesus we meet in the pages of the Gospels has been understood to be the Jesus of history; the Gospels are a valid, authentic, and objective presentation of the Man, His words, and His deeds.

This does not mean that the believing community has not recognized the distinctive flavor of the individual Gospels. Even in the writings of the early church fathers, there is a recognition of the unique emphasis found in the Gospels. But such emphases never were seen as grounds for either suggesting that the Gospel writers were at odds with one another or that they were creatively making things up for some overarching purpose they had in mind in writing what they did. This is not unlike how the eyewitnesses of an accident might all tell the truth about what happened. They indeed witnessed the same event; but due to their particular interests or vantage point, they report on the event with differences in details. The Gospel writers wrote about what Jesus said and did either as eyewitnesses themselves[125] or in direct contact with eyewitnesses.[126]

Both the Scriptures and early church history affirm that there were many eyewitnesses to the life of Jesus. These eyewitnesses, both pro-Christian (e.g., Acts 2:32) and anti-Christian (e.g., Acts 2:22), were alive at the time the oral tradition (such as they might have been) was forming and the initial written account were supposedly prepared. It is historically inconceivable and unreasonable to hold that the creative believing community with the help of theological biased evangelists could have successfully fabricated a "tradition" about Jesus that did not fit the objective, historic truth about Him. The hundreds of eyewitnesses—including those who died for the truth about Him they held to—would hardly have accepted such a fabrication.[127] [128]

For scholars who hold to such a view, the assumption must be made that the early Christian community had a lack of any real interest in preserving sound historical information about Jesus. And yet such scholars readily admit that they desire sound historical information about Jesus, even if they have to "deconstruct" the Gospel records to discover that. Such scholars question the accuracy and reasonable objectivity of the evangelists. They assume that because the Gospels writers were theologically informed and concerned about theological matters, they could not have written accurate history and, instead, resorted to manipulating and creating stories to suit their own views and purposes. What seems to escape the notice of those scholars is that they themselves are theologically informed and concerned in what they pursue. How is it that they presume they are capable of writing and evaluating objectively if the evangelists were incapable?

WHY RAISE THIS ISSUE?

What is the benefit of this short excursus on New Testament criticism? Most who read this volume on the parables of Jesus will not likely find themselves debating such issues within academia. However, because of the influence of the academic world on biblical studies, even a believer who is simply interested in reading and understanding the Bible for himself might bump up against the fruit of such thinking in a seminar, a sermon, or a commentary. As mentioned at the outset, you might hear or read things like this:

- Matthew has altered Mark in this passage by . . .
- These sayings of Jesus were probably not uttered by Jesus in the setting we see here.
- Luke has taken the words of Jesus recorded by Mark and placed them here, in a different setting, to make the point that . . .
- Matthew has created a story that, while reflecting certain truth about Jesus, probably did not happen the way he reports it.
- The Gospel of John is likely the product of a community of people, reflecting on their communal memories of Jesus.

Ideas like these can have a subtle but significant impact on those who read the Gospels. It is that impact, and the implications of that impact, that gives rise to the caution about the fruit of New Testament criticism.

As a reader of the Gospels—and in particular as a reader of Jesus' parables—what might be the benefit of having some understanding of these issues? Let me suggest a few things:

1. Do not naively embrace what comes out of the academic world, even from those you think are theologically conservative. Many believing pastors and teachers

have been trained in seminaries that argue for many of the perspectives of critical theories. That training does have an influence on them. Commentaries written by highly regarded Bible teachers who either teach at or graduated from respected seminaries may still present you arguments that raise questions about the historicity or accuracy of the Gospel accounts. This is not to question either the genuineness of their faith or their sincerity, only to caution against a naïve embracing of all their conclusions and insights.

2. Do approach reading the Gospels as if what you have before you are historically sound and faithful reports of what Jesus said and did. When a Gospel author explains the setting for something that Jesus said, you are free to accept that as it is written. Much like in a courtroom setting, unless there are grounds for raising questions about the veracity of the witness, we grant the assumption of truthfulness to every witness. You should have confidence to read the Gospels with the expectation that you are reading what is true. As we have noticed in these studies on the parables, Jesus' words often "live" in a particular setting. He is responding to certain individuals; He is answering specific questions. And to understand the parables, we should read them as if the setting in which we find them is actually the where and when Jesus taught them.

ENDNOTES

THERE IS A THREE-FOLD PURPOSE to these endnotes. In walking through the parables of Jesus, there are times when some clarification might be needed—not that Jesus is not clear in what He said, but there might be ancillary issues that, if cleared up, will enable us to read well and hear better what He was saying. These endnotes are intended to provide some of that ancillary information that might keep attentive readers from stumbling over things that strike them as unfamiliar or peculiar. By putting such observations in the endnotes, the reading and discussion of the parable itself is left a bit more uncluttered.

There are a few times where some technical clarification of terms or ideas presented in a chapter might be needed or helpful. There might also be some benefit to pointing out additional resources that could help a reader who was interested in digging a bit deeper into some facet of the parable and its exposition. As needed, the endnotes also provide biblical cross references—pointing to other places in the whole of Scripture that touch on what is in view.

1 Even John, the Gospel writer, said that he could not capture all that Jesus said and did (John 21:25).

2 See also Ezekiel 18:4 on the problem of sin.

3 See the prophetic picture of the substitutionary Sacrifice Jesus made as described in Isaiah 53.

4 Although English translation use the words "believe/belief" and "faith/have faith," they actually share the same root and speak of the same thing.

5 Walter Bauer, William F. Arndt, and F. Wilbur Gingrich, *A Greek-English Lexicon of the New Testament and Other Early Christian Literature* (Chicago: University of Chicago Press, 1979), s.v. "παραβολη," 612.

6 R. T. Kendall, *The Parables of Jesus: A Guide to Understanding and Applying the Stories Jesus Taught* (Grand Rapids: Baker, 2008), 14.

7 Simon J. Kistemaker, *The Parables: Understanding the Stories Jesus Told* (Grand Rapids: Baker, 1980), 9.

8 William Barclay, *The Parables of Jesus* (Louisville: Westminster John Knox Press, 1999), 12.

9 The idea of understanding a parable in a fashion similar to how one understands a joke is also discussed in Gordon Fee and Douglas Stuart's *How to Read the Bible for All Its Worth*, 4th ed., (Grand Rapids: Zondervan, 2014), 60-61.

10 For those who need to know, the punch line is as follows: "The string replied, 'No, I'm a frayed knot.'"

11 For those interested in exploring the faithfulness of the Gospel writers in providing their readers with a historically reliable re-telling of the life and ministry of Jesus, see Craig Blomberg, *The Historical Reliability of the Gospels* (Downers Grove: InterVarsity, 1987); Richard Bauckham, *Jesus and the Eyewitnesses* (Grand Rapids: Eerdmans, 2006); and Birger Gerhardsson, *Memory and Manuscript: Oral Transmission and Written Transmission in Rabbinic Judaism and Early Christianity* (Grand Rapids: Eerdmans, 1998).

12 J. Dwight Pentecost, *The Parables of Jesus: Lessons in Life from the Master* (Grand Rapids: Kregel, 1998), 15.

13 Fee and Stuart, *How to Read the Bible*, 60.

14 The parallels to this passage in Matthew on having eyes to see and ears to hear are Mark 4:10-12 and Luke 8:10.

15 We should not shy away from embracing the idea that we might actually have to "think hard" about something we read in Scripture, even if what we are reading are the words of Scripture. Repeatedly, Jesus asked those He spoke with: "Have you never read?" (For example, see Matthew 21:16, 42.) His question implies that they not only could have (and should have) been familiar with the passage to which He was referring, but that the meaning of those texts was not beyond them—but it might require a little thought. In writing to Timothy, Paul said, "Consider what I say, for the Lord will give you understanding" (2 Tim. 2:7). The call to "consider" is a call to think hard, to think well.

16 Julie Andrews, "Do-Re-Mi," Track #8 on *The Sound of Music (Original Soundtrack Recording)*, 20th Century Fox, 1969, compact disc.

17 See, as examples, Mark 3:2; 8:11; Luke 11:16; 23:2 on how the religious teachers were watching Jesus.

18 Read Leviticus 16:29-30, 23:26-32; Numbers 29:7 to learn more about the Day of Atonement. The reference in Acts 27:9 to a fast is also believed by most Bible scholars to be a reference to the Day of Atonement and the surrounding celebration.

19 See Psalm 69:10 on the concept of fasting.

20 Christopher Chabris and Daniel Simons, *The Invisible Gorilla: How Our Intuitions Deceive Us* (New York: Crown Publishing/Random House, 2009).

21 Given Jesus' explanations about the various kinds of soils, some take the approach that this parable is better understood as an allegory. Clearly there is some "one to one" correspondence between the kinds of soil and the kinds of hearers. But being attentive to Jesus' explanation, it might be best to understand Jesus' explanation as only serving to illustrate, rather than to set up a formal allegory. In answering the disciples' question, Jesus pictures various kinds of non-productive soil without, necessarily, seeking to make the story a full allegory. Even when a more allegorical approach is taken to the explanation, the emphasis in the parable is still evident—the

story is about the sower sowing. The active agent is the sower; the soil is not pictured as changing to be more receptive to the seed.

22   When Jesus spoke of the "mystery of the kingdom" (rendered in some translations as "secret"), He was not referring to the idea of mystery the way we might speak of a mystery story or a mystery to be solved. The word refers to something that was not known apart from having it revealed or taught. Although the word only appears in the Gospels in the context of Jesus' telling this parable, the other times in the New Testament where we find this word makes it clear that "mystery" or "secret" is not something to be deduced and figured out but something granted and revealed by God. (For example, see Ephesians 3:1-10, where Paul speaks of God's "mystery.")

23   See Isaiah 6:11-13.

24   Edmond Rostand, *Cyrano de Bergerac,* translated by Brian Vinero (New York City: Broadway Play Publishing, 2023).

25   As described in 2 Kings 24-25 and spoken of by Jeremiah the prophet in Jeremiah 27, 29.

26   The temple rebuilding is recorded in the books of Ezra and Nehemiah.

27   This is what the Samaritan woman Jesus met at the well indicated when she said, "Our fathers worshiped in this mountain, and you people say that in Jerusalem is the place where men ought to worship" (John 4:20).

28   The word used here for "test" is the same word Jesus used in resisting Satan's "temptation," quoting Deuteronomy 6:16, insisting that "you shall not put the Lord your God to the test" (Luke 4:12).

29   The word "Shema" is the first word found in Deuteronomy 6:4 and is often used as a title of a prayer that was used as a central part of the traditional morning and evening prayers for faithful Jews.

30 The call to love God supremely is found throughout the Old Testament; it is at the heart of God's design for His people. See, for example, Deuteronomy 10:12, 30:6; Joshua 23:11; Psalm 31:23.

31 It is worth noting that these two passages—the parable of the "Good Samaritan" and the account of Jesus' exchange with Martha and Mary—

appear only in Luke's Gospel. That they appear here, together, suggests that there is something that the Spirit wants to emphasize through Luke's writing.

32 You can hear Jesus talk about the goodness of God in Matthew 6:25-34 and Luke 12:32.

33 In both the Old Testament and the New Testament, there are examples of people coming to God in prayer in times of need. For example, see Psalm 4:1, 6:9, 66:19-20, 77:1; Micah 7:7; and 2 Corinthians 1:11.

34 For additional study on "the Lord's prayer," see J. I. Packer, *Praying the Lord's Prayer* (Wheaton: Crossway, 2007); W. Phillip Keller, *A Layman Looks at the Lord's Prayer* (Wheaton: Moody, 2017); and Phillip Graham Ryken, *When You Pray: Making the Lord's Prayer Your Own* (Phillipsburg: P & R Publishing, 2006).

35 Jesus describes His own purpose in passages such as Mark 10:44-45 and Luke 4:17-21.

36 Some examples of Jesus' personal time in prayer can be found in Matthew 14:23; Mark 1:35, 6:46; Luke 5:16.

37 You can read about Jesus' moment in prayer at His baptism in Luke 3:21.

38 Luke tells us about Jesus' praying on the Mount of Transfiguration in Luke 9:28-29.

39 Jesus' time of prayer in the Garden of Gethsemane can be found in Luke 22:40-46.

40 Matthew 5:44 and Luke 6:28 record Jesus' instructions about praying for one's enemies.

41 The Scriptures do not condemn the enjoyment of what God bestows on those who are His. See Scriptures such as Ecclesiastes 2:24 and 1 Timothy 6:17.

42 The word for "required" is rather unique. In Luke, this word is found only in this text and in 6:30, where it refers to demanding to have returned something that had been given or loaned. There is, therefore, a subtle implication that the man's soul is "on loan" from God.

43 This word "fool" appears only twice in Luke—here and in 11:40. The word is not speaking about someone who is sinful as much as someone who is lacking in understanding.

44 There is a word that speaks of a fool in a critical or judgmental way—the person who does know better and purposefully ignores what is right. That word is used in places like Matthew 7:26, 23:17 and 2 Timothy 2:23. The other word—the one Jesus uses in this passage—speaks of a foolishness that comes from immaturity or lack of understanding. You will find that word in passages like 1 Corinthians 15:36 and Ephesians 5:17.

45 For examples, see Matthew 5:1-9, 23:27 and Luke 12:56.

46 In referring to those who are "rich," Paul speaks of those who have more than is needed for their daily needs. He is not necessarily referring to people like the multi-millionaires who make the news in our day; he simply might have in mind those who are noticeably better off than others in the community of faith.

47 For a discussion of the "big story of the Bible" idea and its influence on reading Scripture well, please see Appendix C: Thinking About the "Big Story."

48 Luke 4:43, 11:20; Mark 1:14-15; John 8:28-29, 42.

49 In Mark 4:33, we read that Jesus taught His followers "as they were able to hear it."

50 The word rendered "proclaim" in Luke 8:1 and 9:2 does not refer to merely stating something but actually announcing news. The picture that should come to mind is that of the sergeant-at-arms of the Senate, who, when the president is about to step into the House chamber to make his State of the Union Address, proclaims, "Ladies and Gentlemen, the President of the United States."

51 In Luke 10:9, 11, the idea of "coming near" speaks of what is really present. In Luke 11:20, in declaring that His ministry of deliverance meant that the kingdom of God "has come upon" those who are listening to Him, Jesus uses language that means the kingdom has overtaken them.

52 A nearly allegorical and distant future reading of this parable is offered by David Wenham: "The general force of the parable is quite clear: the disciples are servants awaiting their Lord's return, the time of which is unknown"— *The Parables of Jesus* (Downers Grove: InterVarsity, 1989), 77. Others adopt a similar approach. "The focus on these . . . parables is on the unexpectedness of Jesus' future coming . . . In the Gospels we have sayings of Jesus that speak of such a future event . . . in Luke 12:35-48 . . . therefore, it is not difficult to believe that the disciples had already grasped this *parousia* [a future, second coming] concept"—Richard Longnecker, *The Challenge of Jesus' Parables* (Grand Rapids: Eerdmans, 2000), 178, 180. See also J. Dwight Pentecost, *The Parables of Jesus* (Grand Rapids: Kregel, 1982), 81.

53 See, for example, Luke 6:27-36; 9:1-6; 10:1-11, among other passages.

54 Up to this point in Luke, Jesus has only made one reference to Hell in Luke 12:5.

55 Earlier in Luke, we hear Jesus referring to those who—although they had eyes to see all that Jesus was doing and ears to hear all He was teaching—did not truly see (Luke 8:10, 10:24).

56 *The American Heritage Dictionary of the English Language*, s.v. "like" (New York: American Heritage Publishing/Houghton Mifflin, 1973).

57 Although the word "and" does appear in the original text, in a desire to provide a "smoother" English translation, some Bible versions leave out this word.

58 There is a popular view of God's work in rescuing and redeeming us that places an emphasis on God's love for us. It is often expressed in terms of "God does what he does because of His great love for you!" or "Jesus died for you because He didn't want Heaven without you." Although such sentiments rightly affirm God's rich affection for those who are His, the emphasis can, at times, end up skewed. All that God does, He does for His own glory (Isa. 48:11; Ezek. 36:22; Eph. 1:6, 12, 14). We are not the center of the universe for Him; He Himself is at the center of the universe (and the center of His affections). To suggest that God's highest motivation for acting is that He prizes us above all else would mean that God is an idolater—loving something other than God and valuing us as that which is to be supremely

valued. In emphasizing the Lord's genuine and rich affection for those who are His, the goal is not to place us in the center, to make us that which is supreme in the mind and heart of God. Rightly understanding that all God does He does for His own glory does leave room for us to realize that in the pursuit of His own glory He does act in love toward those He redeems—and that love is not a dispassionate, dutiful, begrudging, affection-less love. We are the beneficiaries of God's pursuit of His own glory in that, in so doing, He has set His love (as pictured in this parable) on us.

59 See Paul's request for God to reveal His love fully to the Ephesian Christians in Ephesians 3:18-19.

60 This parable rightly highlights the reason that Jesus pursues those He does—it is for the joy of being with them. As we think about the love God has for us, it is necessary, however, to note that God's love is a discriminating love. That is, God's love for those who are His is substantially different than His love for those who are not (or who are not yet) His own. Although God does pursue His mission in the world because of His great love (John 3:16), those who have not yet come to believe in and depend on the saving work of Jesus are the objects of His wrath (John 3:36; Rom. 1:18-19; Eph. 2:1-3). I would not want to suggest that those who have not yet come to find life in Jesus are the objects of the fullness of God's great love. To affirm that would be to mislead someone who did not yet believe into thinking that, apart from personal faith in Christ Jesus, they were safe and secure in the love of God.

61 For an example, see Jose Gaspar, "Doc Saves Life with Emergency Tracheotomy in Busy Restaurant," Bakersfield Now, September 24, 2013. https://bakersfieldnow.com/news/health/doc-saves-life-with-emergency-tracheotomy-in-busy-restaurant-11-17-2015.

62 See chapter seven on the parable of the man who lost his son.

63 "This [parable] has caused all sorts of problems to commentators. Essentially the problem is: How could the master possibly praise the manager who was so obviously a rogue and who had seriously defrauded him?"—David Wenham, *The Parables of Jesus* (Downers Grove: InterVarsity Press, 1968), 163. "This parable, of which the difficulties are exceedingly great has been the

subject of manifold, and those the most opposite, interpretations"—R. C. Trench, *Notes on the Parables of Our Lord* (Grand Rapids: Baker, 1979), 153).

64 Luke 6:12-49

65 Luke 9:1-11

66 Luke 9:46-52

67 Luke 12:1-34

68 This word for "squandered" is only used a few times in the New Testament. A sense for the word is seen when Jesus spoke about what would happen when He was arrested and taken away: His followers would be "scattered" (Matt. 26:31; Mark 14:27). In Luke 15:13, this is also the word used for how the "prodigal son" wasted all he had received from his father.

69 The first time, the word appears in adverb form, the only time the adverb is used in the New Testament. The other time the adjective form of the word is used; that word appears a little over a dozen times in the New Testament.

70 The other word used in the New Testament that is translated as "wise" (Greek *sophos, sophia*; appearing a little over seventy times), carries more a sense of being skilled or living life in an appropriate and competent way.

71 The expression "unrighteous wealth" is the rendering of two words. The first speaks of that which is not right, acceptable, just. The other word (rendered "wealth") is found only in this passage and related parallel passages in the Gospels. It carries a sense of not simply money (i.e., one's cash on hand or savings in the bank) but anything that might be construed as valuable—thus, the reason why we are picturing it as unrighteous "stuff."

72 Although the Old Testament did have some large divisions in the books, our present chapter and verse divisions were a later addition to the biblical text. For more information on chapter and verse divisions in the Bible, see https://www.biblegateway.com/blog/2016/12/where-do-verse-and-chapter-numbers-come-from.

73 Some Bible teachers suggest that by making the statement that "there is only One who is good," Jesus is making a claim to be God. That, however, seems quite unlikely, given that Jesus does not seem to be concerned about

asserting His identity in this exchange and recognizing that if this was an attempt to assert His Divinity, it is a very ambiguous way of doing so.

74 Exodus 20:1-17; Deuteronomy 5:6–21.

75 There is a widely touted explanation of this short parable about a gate in the city of Jerusalem called the "eye of the needle." Reportedly, this gate was so small that if someone sought entrance with a pack camel, the load would have to be removed and the camel made to crouch or crawl through the gate. Thus, it would be quite hard, but not impossible, to get a camel through the "eye of the needle." Some say this pictures the humility needed in approaching life with God. As widespread as this explanation is, there does not appear to be any reliable archeological evidence that such a gate existed in Jesus' day. Some Bible teachers have even been known to show pictures of the (supposed) "eye of the needle" gate; but do not forget those pictures were not taken in Jesus' day!

76 A denarius was the average wage paid to a day laborer.

77 The third hour would be nine o'clock in the morning.

78 Noon and 3:00 p.m., respectively.

79 Five o'clock in the afternoon.

80 See Brian Onken, *More Than His God Card* (Greenville: Ambassador International, 2014) for a fuller explanation of this idea.

81 With the feast underway, the pilgrims arriving in Jerusalem would have been singing songs as they traveled to the city. That gives a rich setting to Jesus' arrival, as their hope that Jesus might be the promised Messiah mixes with the joyous celebrating of the feast.

82 Jesus was aware that the crowd's celebration, sincere as it might have been, was not fully informed and that it would only be a short while before His crucifixion and death would alter the joyful response of the gathered crowd.

83 See Jeremiah 7:11 and Isaiah 56:6-7.

84 This was apparently a formal delegation, either sent by or consisting of

members of the Sanhedrin—the Jewish ruling council with some measure of governmental power granted by Rome.

85 Simon Kistemaker wrote that in this parable, "Jesus implied that he was the personification of the landowner's son . . . Thus Jesus spoke of his imminent death and impending exaltation"—*The Parables* (Grand Rapids: Baker, 1980), 88. In similar fashion, David Wenham explained, "The parable makes clear that Jesus sees his own death as the climax of the people's rejection of God's invitation to them to fulfill their proper role"—*The Parables of Jesus* (Downers Grove: InterVarsity, 1989), 127.

86 Notice that Luke does not simply tell us that Jesus replied to those who reacted to the parable; He looked directly at them as He replied.

87 Jesus also appears to draw on Isaiah 8:14-15 in saying what He did. Although it is not a direct quote, He does seem to allude to that idea found there.

88 I believe I was first introduced to this expression by Becky Manley Pippert, an InterVarsity campus staff member I heard speak when I was in college.

89 Luke, similarly, reported, "The scribes and the chief priests tried to lay hands on Him that very hour, and they feared the people; for they understood that He spoke this parable against them" (Luke 20:19).

90 Although the idea of Jesus being the groom and the Church being His bride is found later in the Scriptures (see Rev. 19:7, 9 and Eph. 5:25), at this point of Jesus' self-revelation, it would not have been something clear to His hearers.

91 The sense of "paid no attention" is more than just they overlooked or missed the invitation being extended. They neglected what they knew.

92 In the New Testament, particularly in Paul's letters, the idea of "called" often carries the sense of God's electing purposes in redeeming people and adopting them into His family (see, for example, Rom. 8:29-30; 1 Cor. 1:23-24; 2 Tim. 1:9). But that does not appear to be what Jesus has in mind in telling this parable. The word rendered "call" in verse three is also translated "invite" or "invited" four times in this parable.

93 There are a couple of words that could be translated "evil" in the Gospels.

The word used in this parable is commonly used to refer to something or someone that brings an evil, malignant presence.

94 The core idea behind the word is that of "playing a role" and, in the Greek culture of the day, would have been used in a less critical way in speaking of actors on the stage who projected an image that was not them. When used by Jesus (fifteen times in Matthew), He is speaking of those who are disingenuous and lacking integrity or sincerity in what they are pursuing.

95 "Some purist is likely to insist that the text does not explicitly call this passage a parable"—Dale Ralph Davis, *Luke 14-24: On the Road the Jerusalem* (Geanies: Christian Focus Publications, 2021), 49. "Because of the name 'Lazarus,' it has been suggested that 16:19-31 is not a parable but a historical account"—Robert Stein, *Luke*, NAC (Nashville: B & H Publishing, 1992), 422.

96 For example, see Matthew 13:24, 31, 21:33; Luke 12:16, 13:6, 20:9. "Within the Gospel [of Luke] are seven instances in which an account begins 'a certain man.' In all but one (14:2) this was used to introduce a parable (10:30; 14:16; 15:11; 16:1; 16:19; 19:12). The last six examples are furthermore introduced by 'he [Jesus] said/was saying' whereas 14:2 is clearly part of a narrative. This account also beings with the same introduction as the parable in 16:1, 'There was a rich man,' so Luke intended for his readers to interpret this as a parable, not as a historical account"—Robert Stein, *Luke*, NAC (Nashville: B & H Publishing, 1992), 422.

97 Although David Wenham does treat this story as a parable, he notes, "Nowhere else in any of Jesus' parables are the actors in the stories named."—David Wenham, *The Parables of Jesus* (Downers Grove: InterVarsity Press, 1989), 143.

98 Wenham, *The Parables of Jesus*, 143.

99 "The picture of Lazarus in bliss and of the rich man in torment with a chasm between them is a vivid one. But it should be understood as pictorial rather than as anything like a literal description of heaven and hell"—David Wenham, *The Parables of Jesus* (Downers Grove: InterVarsity Press, 1989), 144.

100 This is in contrast to Jesus' parable of "The Good Samaritan," where, in that story, we are specifically told of those who noticed the man who had been beaten and robbed and purposefully passed by him.

101 See, for example, Genesis 13:1-6.

102 The word "Hades" that appears in this text is only found ten times in the New Testament. The basic sense of the word appears to be "where the dead are," without specifying the kind of distinctions between Heaven and Hell common in Christian theology. See Robert Stein, *Luke*, NAC (Nashville: B & H Publishing, 1992), 424.

103 The expression "Abraham's bosom" is unique, in that it only appears here in Bible. It is "A figure of speech used by Jesus . . . The dead Lazarus is portrayed as reclining next to Abraham"—*New Bible Dictionary*, 3rd ed. (Downers Grove: InterVarsity Press, 1996), s.v. "Abraham's Bosom," 8.

104 Although it is not uncommon to suggest that the reference to someone coming back from the dead is pointing ahead to Jesus' resurrection, that is not evident in the account. It is a fascinating side note to observe that after the resurrection of Lazarus in John 11, those opposed to Jesus did not change their minds about Him in light of "someone coming back from the dead." In fact, they determined to kill the man who was raised (see John 12:10-11)!

105 See the discussion in the introductory chapter on understanding parables.

106 The Greek particle used here (*de*) can be translated "but, and, now." It is commonly seen as introducing an explanatory comment or extending the previous thought. See, for example, Luke 16:1 ("*Now* He was also saying"); 16:4 ("*Now* the Pharisees, who were lovers of money"); 16:15 (*But* God knows your hearts"); 16:17 ("*But* it is easier").

107 To refer to "the Law and the Prophets" is fundamentally the same as speaking of "Moses and the Prophets" as we find in the parable. Both are ways of referring to the Scriptures that the Jews in Jesus' day would have known.

108 The idea is that people are "forcing their way into the kingdom of God, a plea for moral enthusiasm and spiritual passion and energy"—A. T. Robertson, *Word Pictures in the New Testament*, vol. 2 (Grand Rapids: Baker), 220.

109 See, for example, Matthew 5:31-32; 19:3-7; Mark 2:10-12.

110 Some of the religious leaders of the day might have claimed that because they were related to "father Abraham" that their standing with God was

assured (Matt. 3:9; Luke 3:8). But to think of Abraham as one's national "father" does not resolve the "two masters" problem.

111 R. C. Trench, *Notes on the Parables of Our Lord* ([Grand Rapids: Baker Book House, 1979), 162.

112 Trench, 162.

113 See Acts 17:11 and 2 Timothy 2:15 for great examples of the importance of personal attentiveness.

114   Paul encourages his readers to reflect deeply and with thoughtful intention on his words in Ephesians 3:4 and 2 Timothy 2:7. He says that by reflecting back on things he has said and written, they will "understand [his] insight into the mystery of Christ" (Eph. 3:4). This suggests that he anticipated they might have to think about what they have heard and learned from him as they press on to understand what he goes on to tell them. When he wrote to Timothy, Paul also addressed the need to think well about what one reads and hears. With regard to what he had written, he told Timothy to "consider what I say, for the Lord will give you understanding in everything" (2 Tim. 2:7). Although it is clear that Paul knows the Lord will help Timothy to understand truth, he still calls him to "consider." The word implies giving thoughtful attention to what is Paul had communicated; Timothy will need to think well.

115 2 Timothy 3:16; 2 Peter 1:20-21.

116   John 14:26; John 16:13; 1 Corinthians 2:10-16. There are a number of passages that point to the Spirit's help in the reading and understanding of truth. Speaking to His disciples, Jesus said the Spirit would teach them (John 14:26) and that the Spirit would guide them into truth (John 16:13). They would not be on their own to simply "figure out" what they needed to know. In his letter to the Corinthians, Paul noted that he could write those believers about spiritual truth because the Spirit had been given to them and He would enable them to grasp Gospel truth (1 Cor. 2:10-16).

117   Paul encourages believers to allow Gospel truth to fill them so that it overflows in teaching and building one another up (Col. 3:16; 1 Thess. 1:8; 2 Thess. 3:1; Eph. 4:11-16).

118 *Forrest Gump*, directed by Robert Zemeckis (1994; Savannah, GA: Paramount Pictures).

119 For an introduction and review of the most common perspectives on resolving the Synoptic Problem, see Robert L. Thomas, ed., *Three Views on the Origins of the Synoptic Gospels* (Grand Rapids: Kregel, 2002). For a more in-depth exploration of roots of the Synoptic Problem, see Eta Linnemann, *Is There a Synoptic Problem?*, trans. Robert Yarborough (Grand Rapids: Baker Book House; 1992). For a theologically conservative critique of the fruit of New Testament Criticism, see Robert L. Thomas and F. David Farnell, eds., *The Jesus Crisis* (Grand Rapids: Kregel, 1998).

120 Martin Dibelius, *From Tradition to Gospel* (New York: Charles Scribner's Sons, n.d.).

121 Rudolph Bultmann, *The History of the Synoptic Tradition*, trans. Edwin Leverenz and Rudolf Nordin (St. Louis: Concordia, 1977).

122 Bultmann, *Jesus Christ and Mythology* (New York: Charles Scribner's Sons, 1958).

123 "Across the whole field of New Testament studies from mid-century to the present day, skepticism [regarding the historicity of the Gospels] has proven to be a stubborn, if not ineradicable, habit of mind"—Ben. F. Meyer, "Some Consequences of Birger Gerhardsson's Account of the Origins of the Gospel Tradition," in *Jesus and the Oral Gospel Tradition*, ed. Henry Wansbrough (New York: T & T Clark, 2044), 428.

124 For an in-depth defense of the reliable eyewitness nature of the Gospels, see Meyer, "Some Consequences;" Birger Gerhardsson, *Memory and Manuscript and Tradition and Transmission in Early Christianity* (Grand Rapids: Eerdmans, 1998); Richard Bauckham, *Jesus and the Eyewitnesses* (Grand Rapids: Eerdmans, 2006).

125 Notice, for example, John 20:30; 21:24-25.

126 See Luke 1:1-4.

127 Fritz Rienecker, *Das Evangelium des Matthaus*, Wuppertaler Studienbible Reihi NT, 9th ed., (1977), 3-4.

128 Eta Linnemann, *Is There a Synoptic Problem?* trans. Robert Yarborough (Grand Rapids: Baker Book House; 1992), 185.

BIBLIOGRAPHY

American Heritage Dictionary of the English Language, The. New York: American Heritage Publishing/Houghton Mifflin, 1973.

Andrews, Julie. "Do-Re-Mi." *The Sound of Music (Original Soundtrack Recording).* 20th Century Fox, 1969. Compact disc.

Barclay, William. *The Parables of Jesus.* Louisville: Westminster John Knox Press, 1999.

Bauckham, Richard. "The Rich Man and Lazarus: The Parable and the Parallels." *New Testament Studies* 37: 1991.

Bauckham, Richard. *Jesus and the Eyewitnesses.* Grand Rapids: Eerdmans, 2006.

Bauer, Walter, William F. Arndt, and F. Wilbur Gingrich. *A Greek-English Lexicon of the New Testament and Other Early Christian Literature.* Chicago: University of Chicago Press, 1979.

Blomberg, Craig. *The Historical Reliability of the Gospels.* Downers Grove: InterVarsity, 1987.

Bultmann, Rudolph. *Jesus Christ and Mythology.* New York: Charles Scribner's Sons, 1958.

Bultmann, Rudolph. *The History of the Synoptic Tradition*. Translated by Edwin Leverenz and Rudolf Nordin. St. Louis: Concordia, 1977.

Buttrick, George. *The Parables of Jesus*. New York: Doubleday, 1928.

Chabris, Christopher, and Daniel Simons. *The Invisible Gorilla: How Our Intuitions Deceive Us*. New York: Crown Publishing/ Random House, 2009.

Davis, Dale Ralph. *Luke 14-24: On the Road the Jerusalem*. Geanies, Scotland: Christian Focus Publications, 2021.

Dibelius, Martin. *From Tradition to Gospel*. New York: Charles Scribner's Sons, n.d.

Dumas, Alexander. *The Count of Monte Cristo*. Translated by Robin Buss. New York: Penguin, 1996.

Fee, Gordon and Douglas Stuart. *How to Read the Bible for All Its Worth*. 4th ed. Grand Rapids: Zondervan, 2014.

Gerhardsson, Birger. *Memory and Manuscript: Oral Transmission and Written Transmission in Rabbinic Judaism and Early Christianity*. Grand Rapids: Eerdmans, 1998.

Hendricks, Howard, and William D. Hendricks. "What Type of Literature is This?" in *Living by the Book*. Chicago: Moody Press, 1990.

Gaspar, Jose. "Doc Saves Life with Emergency Tracheotomy in Busy Restaurant." Bakersfield Now. September 24, 2013. https://bakersfieldnow.com/news/health/doc-saves-life-with-emergency-tracheotomy-in-busy-restaurant-11-17-2015.

Forrest Gump, directed by Robert Zemeckis (1994; Savannah, GA: Paramount Pictures).

Keller, W. Phillip. *A Layman Looks at the Lord's Prayer.* Wheaton: Moody, 2017.

Kendall, R. T. *The Parables of Jesus: A Guide to Understanding and Applying the Stories Jesus Taught.* Grand Rapids: Baker, 2008.

Kistemaker, Simon. *The Parables: Understanding the Stories Jesus Told.* Grand Rapids: Baker, 1980.

Linnemann, Eta. *Is There a Synoptic Problem?* Translated by Robert Yarborough. Grand Rapids: Baker Book House; 1992.

Longnecker, Ricard. *The Challenge of Jesus' Parables.* Grand Rapids: Eerdmans, 2000.

Marshall, I. Howard, A. R. Millard, J. I. Packer, D. J. Wiseman, eds. *New Bible Dictionary,* 3rd ed. Downers Grove, Ill.: InterVarsity Press, 1996.

Meyer, Ben F. "Some Consequences of Birger Gerhardsson's Account of the Origins of the Gospel Tradition." *Jesus and the Oral Gospel Tradition.* Ed. Henry Wansbrough. New York: T & T Clark, 2004.

Onken, Brian. *More Than His God Card.* Greenville: Ambassador International, 2014.

Packer, J. I. *Praying the Lord's Prayer.* Wheaton: Crossway, 2007.

Pentecost, J. Dwight. *The Parables of Jesus: Lessons in Life from the Master.* Grand Rapids: Zondervan, 1982. Reprint, Grand Rapids, Mich.: Kregel, 1998.

Pentecost, J. Dwight. *The Parables of Jesus*. Grand Rapids: Kregel, 1982.

Rienecker, Fritz. *Das Evangelium des Matthaus*. Wuppertaler Studienbible Reihi NT, 9th ed. 1977.

Robertson, A. T. *Word Pictures in the New Testament*. 6 vols. Grand Rapids: Baker Book House, n.d.

Ryken, Phillip Graham. *When You Pray: Making the Lord's Prayer Your Own*. Phillipsburg: P & R Publishing, 2006.

Stein, Robert H. *An Introduction to the Parables of Jesus*. Philadelphia: Westminster Press, 1981.

Stein, Robert. *Luke*. NAC. Nashville: B & H Publishing, 1992.

Thayer, Joseph. *Greek-English Lexicon of the New Testament*. Peabody: Hendrickson, 2000.

Thomas, Robert L. and F. David Farnell, eds. *The Jesus Crisis*. Grand Rapids: Kregel, 1998.

Thomas, Robert L., ed. *Three Views on the Origins of the Synoptic Gospels*. Grand Rapids: Kregel, 2002.

Trench, R. C. *Notes on the Parables of Our Lord*. Grand Rapids: Baker, 1979.

Wenham, David. *The Parables of Jesus*. Downers Grove: InterVarsity Press, 1968.

ABOUT THE AUTHOR

BRIAN IS A BIBLE TEACHER, first and foremost. He is committed to helping others encounter Jesus, as He is presented in the Scriptures, for their ever-increasing joy in Him. With over thirty years of pastoral and teaching experience and holding advanced degrees in both New Testament studies and theology, Brian brings a scholar's vision and a disciple's passion to this study of Jesus' parables.

For more information about
Brian Onken
and
More Than A Clever Story
please visit:

www.theriverupstate.org
www.facebook.com/TheRiverUpstate

Brian can be reached at
brianonken55@gmail.com

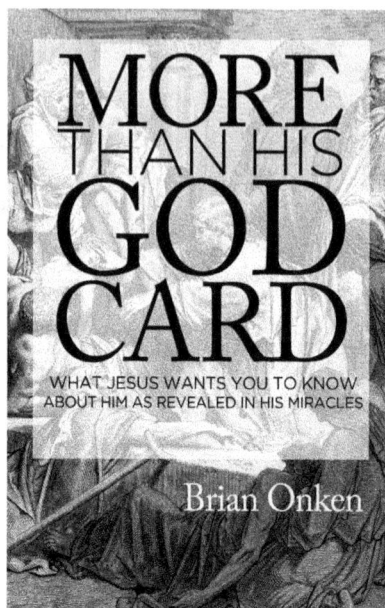

MORE THAN HIS GOD CARD

WHAT JESUS WANTS YOU TO KNOW
ABOUT HIM AS REVEALED IN HIS MIRACLES

Brian Onken

Many readers of the Bible assume that when Jesus did a miracle it was, fundamentally, to prove that He was God—Jesus was pulling out His "God Card." What is startling is that Jesus never made the case that this was the primary purpose of His miracles.

What if Jesus was intending to reveal something different, something more, something beyond merely proving His identity? Seeing as Jesus' miracles were such a significant part of His ministry, if we miss what His miracles do reveal, we may be missing out on great insights into the One who loves us and came to rescue us.

Like the restoration of a great Old Master's painting, Brian leads his readers to a fresh vision of what is conveyed in the Gospel accounts of Jesus' miracles. Uncovering what is there, in the text, we see the miracles in a reinvigorated, vibrant way. You will never read about the miracles in the same way . . . and you will catch a renewed and compelling glimpse of Jesus.

AVAILABLE FROM YOUR FAVORITE RETAILER.

For more information about
Brian Onken
and
More Than A Clever Story
please visit:

www.theriverupstate.org
www.facebook.com/TheRiverUpstate

Brian can be reached at
brianonken55@gmail.com

Ambassador International's mission is to magnify the Lord Jesus Christ and promote His Gospel through the written word.

We believe through the publication of Christian literature, Jesus Christ and His Word will be exalted, believers will be strengthened in their walk with Him, and the lost will be directed to Jesus Christ as the only way of salvation.

For more information about
AMBASSADOR INTERNATIONAL
please visit:

www.ambassador-international.com
@AmbassadorIntl
www.facebook.com/AmbassadorIntl

Thank you for reading this book!

You make it possible for us to fulfill our mission, and we are grateful for your partnership.

To help further our mission, please consider leaving us a review on your social media, favorite retailer's website, Goodreads or Bookbub, or our website, and make sure to check out the books on the following page.

More from Ambassador International

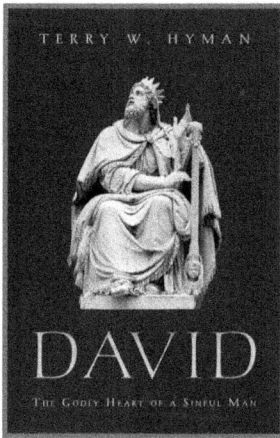

To some people, saying David had a godly heart is almost offensive. How do you apply that description to a man whose legacy includes neglecting responsibilities, lust, adultery, murder, deception, hypocrisy, and callous indifference? *David: The Godly Heart of a Sinful Man* examines David's heart, identifying specific character qualities that influenced his response when confronted with his sin.

Job is well-known, even in the public arena. However, the main character of the book is the Triune God. Moreover, some have suggested the book of Job focuses on the larger problem of evil in a good God's world. By definition that would include the concept of victimhood. However, Dr. Jim Halla thinks that approach misses major issues. *The Book of Job: God's Faithfulness in Troubled Times* presents an in depth look into Job and how it applies to the New Testament, Jesus, and us.

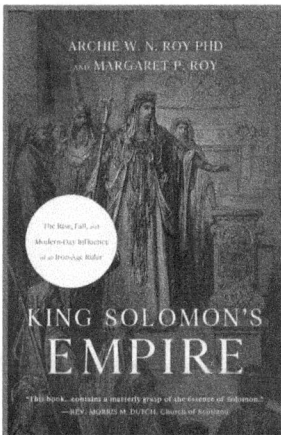

King Solomon is known as the wisest and richest man to have ever lived, but who was this man really? Even though we read his words in the Bible, this man who was the son of "the man after God's own heart" remains a mystery. Even his death is veiled in conspiracy theories. How could a man who was granted his greatest wish by God Himself be so enamored with the pleasures of this world—hungry for sex, power, and more wealth? In *King Solomon's Empire*, Archie and Margaret Roy take an in-depth look into the life of the wise king and the kingdom he led.

www.ingramcontent.com/pod-product-compliance
Lightning Source LLC
Chambersburg PA
CBHW051415090426
42737CB00014B/2672

with such restaurants, the food was cooked on a large grill in the middle of the table in front of the diners. Our particular chef was pleasant enough, but he was not skilled in the art of teppanyaki-style cooking. There was very little show, little artistic flair. But all in all, the food was good and a nice change of pace—that is, until dessert.

When we were asked if we would like dessert, we anticipated something that would fit with a Japanese steak house. In previous experiences, the most common offering would have been green tea ice cream. But to our surprise, we were offered something else: deep-fried ice cream.

Now for those who have never visited Mexico or frequented a Mexican restaurant, that is a common (and tasty!) confection. But it just does not fit with a Japanese meal. When you go to an Italian eatery for dinner, you expect bread and olive oil—you would be surprised if the wait staff brought you chips and salsa to nibble on as you waited for your meal. And how disappointing it would be if you were in a Mexican restaurant and they informed you—upon asking—that they do not have chips or salsa. Some things just go together!

Sometimes when we are reading Scripture, we come across a somewhat familiar passage. Perhaps we have heard someone teach on the passage before; maybe we have come across the text in a devotional book. We can easily slip into thinking, "I know what this is about." If we are not careful, we might end up overlooking how that passage is actually supposed to fit in the context in which we find it. We end up thinking "Italian bread" when it is really a "chips and salsa" passage.